PENGUIN BOOKS

1066: THE YEAR OF THE CONQUEST

David Howarth is a distinguished naval and military historian whose accounts of Trafalgar and Waterloo are now regarded as classics. Called by *The New Yorker* "a brilliant writer full of grace, wit and common sense," he is also the author of *The Voyage of the Armada*, *Tahiti*, and *Lord Nelson*, written with (his son) Stephen Howarth.

D1363635

1066
The Year of the Conquest

DAVID HOWARTH

Illustrations to chapter headings by
GARETH FLOYD

PENGUIN BOOKS

PENGUIN BOOKS
Published by the Penguin Group
Penguin Books USA Inc.,
375 Hudson Street, New York, New York 10014, U.S.A.
Penguin Books Ltd, 27 Wrights Lane, London W8 5TZ, England
Penguin Books Australia Ltd, Ringwood, Victoria, Australia
Penguin Books Canada Ltd, 10 Alcorn Avenue,
Toronto, Ontario, Canada M4V 3B2
Penguin Books (N.Z.) Ltd, 182–190 Wairau Road, Auckland 10, New Zealand

Penguin Books Ltd, Registered Offices:
Harmondsworth, Middlesex, England

First published in the United States of America by
Viking Penguin Inc. 1978
Published in Penguin Books 1981

23 22

LIBRARY OF CONGRESS CATALOGING IN PUBLICATION DATA
Howarth, David Armine, 1912–
1066: the year of the conquest.
Reprint. Originally published: New York:
Viking Press, 1978.
Bibliography: p.
Includes index.
1. Great Britain—History—Norman period, 1066–
1154. 2. Hastings, Battle of, 1066. I. Title.
[DA195.H69 1981] 942.02′1 81-1816
ISBN 0 14 00.5850 8 AACR2

Printed in the United States of America
Set in Monotype Bembo

Contents

Maps and Diagrams

Introduction

A few years ago I wrote a book about Waterloo and one about Trafalgar, and tried to describe those battles from the points of view of men who fought in them. Here I have tried to do the same thing with the year 1066: not only its battles, but also the peaceful life that the battles disrupted, and not only its kings and dukes and earls, but also its humble people.

1066 is the date that English people remember from history lessons at school long after they have forgotten all the others. But this book is not about the historical importance of the year, it is simply about the tremendous drama that began on January 6 with the burial of King Edward in Westminster Abbey, and ended on Christmas Day in the same place with the coronation of King William. The people who witnessed the drama could not foresee its historical results, so the results have no proper place in the telling of it, except as a postscript.

Like those other books, this is not meant to be read as a work of scholarship, only as an evocation of the excitement, pleasures and miseries of that year; but I hope it is accurate enough to satisfy scholars. There is an obvious difference in going so much farther back in history: there are not so many contemporary sources. But there are more than one might expect. This account of the year is based on twenty others, of which twelve were written within living memory of 1066, and all except two within a hundred years. Many of them are mentioned in the story, and there is a list of them all with their dates on page 202.

A less obvious difference is that all the early accounts are more or less prejudiced. Immediately after 1066, there were naturally three different versions of what had happened, Norman, English and Scandinavian. The rather later writers added new stories, either from earlier versions which are lost or from oral traditions, and these already had the quality of legends when they were written. Moreover, most of the writers were monks who felt bound to draw moral conclusions, and some were writing for patrons who expected their own opinions to be confirmed.

So any modern historian has to use his own judgement pretty freely. When he finds contradictory stories, he has to decide which is most probable, which writer had the best reason to know the truth – or which, on the other hand, had reason to distort it; and if he cannot decide, he has to tell all the versions. On the whole, all the early writers were more likely to be right about things in their own country, and were sometimes obviously wrong about things in other countries; so one tends to accept Norman stories about Normandy, English ones about England and Norse ones about Norway. Apart from that, I think it is fair to say that Normans were the least reliable, because they felt they had to make excuses for their invasion, and their writers were sometimes deceived by their own propaganda.

Strictly speaking, every sentence in a story nine centuries old should include the word *perhaps*: nothing is perfectly certain. But that would be boring, and I have left out the qualification whenever things seem reasonably certain, either from the early sources or from deduction and inference. After all, factual truth is not the only thing that matters. It can be just as illuminating to know what people thought or pretended was true, if one can discover why they thought it, or why they had to pretend it. I do not despise a plausible legend, or totally disbelieve a miracle that everyone believed in. Sometimes I have made guesses, but not without saying so.

Better scholars might say I have gone too far in trying to draw the characters of the people of 1066; but I think this is the most enjoyable part of history. To understand the things these people did, one has to do one's best to understand the psychological reasons why they did them. Why, for one example, did William of Normandy ever contemplate the invasion of England? It seems far too risky an action for any intelligent military man to take through greed, or lust for power, or revenge. I have suggested a more compelling reason which I think rings true. And why did King

Harold appear to behave quite differently at Stamford Bridge and at Hastings three weeks later?

Obviously one ought to be careful in using one's understanding of modern people, such as it is, to interpret the actions of people so long ago. Their beliefs were somewhat simpler than ours, their knowledge was far more limited, their lives were subject less to law and more to custom. Christian ethics were more a set of rules demanded by the church, and less an inborn habit of mind; accepted morals were stricter in some ways and more easy-going in others.

Yet so far as one can tell, their minds worked in just the same way. Their thoughts were no more illogical than most of ours, and their emotions were identical, though less inhibited. Sometimes they acted in charity and hope, sometimes in envy and fear, and often in the muddle of motives which is familiar to us all.

So I think it is possible, using every scrap of information, to make a worth-while portrait of each of the leading actors in the drama. On the other hand, it is impossible to judge them by the standards of their own time and unfair to judge them by ours; the only acceptable judgement is that of their friends and countrymen. We ought not to take sides in their passionate arguments – nor do we need to, because all of them are equally our ancestors and there is something of all their characters in each of us.

But thinking about them as the kind of men and women one might meet and know, one begins to like some of them more than others; and why not? Personally, I think that if I had been around at the time I would have liked King Harold, heartily disliked King Edward the Confessor, felt sorry for Earl Tostig and terrified of Duke William, and found nothing whatever to say to King Harald Hardrada of Norway. I have not tried to hide this blatant prejudice, but I hope my portraits are fair enough to let anyone else disagree with me.

England

New Year's Day

It was not a bad life to be English when the year began; it was the kind of life that many modern people vainly envy. For the most part, it was lived in little villages, and it was almost completely self-sufficient and self-supporting: the only things most villages had to buy or barter were salt and iron. Of course it was a life of endless labour, as any simple life must be, but the labour was rewarded: there was plenty to eat and drink, and plenty of space, and plenty of virgin land for ambitious people to clear and cultivate. And of course the life had sudden alarms and dangers, as human life has had in every age, but they were less frequent than they had ever been: old men remembered the ravages of marauding armies, but for two generations the land had been at peace. Peace had made it prosperous, taxes had been reduced; people had a chance to be a little richer than their forefathers. Even the weather was improving. For a long time, England had been wetter and colder than it normally is, but it was entering a phase which lasted two centuries when the summers were unusually warm and sunny and the winters mild. Crops flourished, and men and cattle throve. Most of the English were still very poor, but most of the comforts they lacked were things they had never heard of.

In trying to recall that life, the most striking thing, especially to a modern Englishman, is its isolation. For every person who lived in England then there are forty now. In terms of population, the towns were negligible. London was unique, with twelve to fifteen thousand people; York may have had eight thousand, and a dozen others from fifteen hundred to four thousand. All in all, perhaps one Englishman in twenty might have called himself a townsman; the other nineteen were villagers.

A village was surrounded by a fence, and its land by another outer fence. Beyond that were miles and miles of primeval forest and heath, empty and wild, where men would venture by day to herd their pigs or gather logs for winter, but would not willingly spend the night for fear of wolves and spirits. Tracks for ponies led through the wilderness to other villages, winding among the thickets and marshy places and fording the streams. Somewhere, the tracks joined a road the Romans had built at least six hundred years before, grass-grown and neglected ever since; and somewhere even more remote, the road reached one of the little stockaded towns. It was said of that time of peace that even a woman with a baby could safely travel alone the length and breadth of England. But it would have been a very adventurous journey for anyone, safe enough perhaps from human enemies, but with untold dangers of accident or sickness far from home, or simply of losing the way. Nobody but the high and mighty with their escorts, or their messengers, or a few travelling merchants, had any compelling reason to try it. King Edward himself, who had reigned for twenty-four years, had never gone to the northern half of his kingdom. For ordinary people, to see the nearest town might be the event of a year or even a lifetime, and to meet a stranger was a nine days' wonder. If a traveller approached the village, he blew a horn before he crossed the outer fence to show he was coming openly.

Within his own village, an Englishman knew everybody and almost every tree and animal. He knew his rights and duties, the favours he could ask of his neighbours and the favours he could offer in return. He knew the view from the tops of the nearest hills, and the tracks to the neighbouring villages, and from the sun he knew the direction of things, the north, south, east and west. He thought of himself and everyone he knew as English, and of England as the demesne of English kings, surrounded by sea except where the faraway hostile lands of Wales and Scotland joined it. But he had no conception of a map, no mental image of the shape of the country as it might be seen from hundreds of miles above, or of the relative positions of places in it. He lived in a world that had his own village as its centre. His image of England was the view from the village, the tracks that led away in each direction to impenetrable distances, ever mistier, vaguer and more daunting. With such an outlook, the village must have had an intense quality of homeliness that only the simplest people can experience.

Conversely, the news of the outside world that came into the village was vague, brought by pedlars, or filtering down from mouth to mouth from the house of the lord, or rumoured at the occasional district meetings. The great events of the time were written down by monks in their chronicles and so became history; but to the men and women who were living in the villages of England then, they were only oral tales of distant happenings, more or less twisted in the telling. Battles, the deaths of kings and rivalries of earls, were only important if they seemed to threaten the stable tenor of the village life, and the mutual kindness and custom that held it together; or worst of all, if they suddenly threatened to bring ferocious strangers tramping through the place, burning and slaughtering like the Danish and Norwegian Vikings in the bad old days.

It was those depredations in the past, more than anything else, that had given England the social structure it had in 1066. It was a farming country, land was its absorbing interest; and originally, plots of land had been owned outright by the men who settled and cleared them, and inherited by their children. But such independent farmers had no defence against the Viking raids, or resources to tide them over other disasters like cattle sickness, a series of bad harvests, fire or storm. In the course of time, almost every man in the country had attached himself by mutual promises to somebody more powerful, who could help to protect him and his family in times of stress. Small landowners had surrendered the nominal ownership of their land to their protectors – who in turn held the land in duty to somebody higher. This evolution has often been called a loss of freedom, and so it was; but absolute personal freedom had come to be, as perhaps it has always been, a dangerous illusion. Its loss was really a gain: the acceptance of the duties and mutual support of a social system, the end of anarchy.

By 1066, the system was elaborate and stable. There were many social strata. At the bottom were serfs or slaves; next cottagers or cottars; then villeins, who farmed as much perhaps as fifty acres; then thanes, who drew rents in kind from the villeins; then earls, each ruling one of the six great earldoms that covered the country; and above all, the King. And in parallel to this secular social ladder was the hierarchy of the church, from village priests to archbishops. None of these people could claim the absolute ownership of land. The villeins, to use the old phrase, 'held their land of' the thanes, the thanes held it of an earl or the church or the King, and the King held it all of God's grace. And each of them, without exception, owed duties to the others above and below him. Of course, the system and the people were fallible and the duties were not always done; but it was the clear intention of the English that they should be done. The law gave remedies, and nobody in theory was above it. Only three months before the year began, the Earl of Northumbria had been rejected by his thanes who thought he had failed in his duty to them; and the King had had to send him into exile and give them the earl they wanted. Even the King himself could be dethroned.

It is hard to describe any social system in general terms; the generalities get lost among all the special cases and exceptions. Besides, most people do not have to understand the whole of the social system they live under, only the bits of it that happen to affect them. For this ancient system, it is more illuminating to choose one ordinary village and see how the system appeared to the people who were living there on that New Year's Day. With all England to choose from, I have picked the village of Horstede in Sussex – because, for one reason, it lay uncomfortably near the scene of the final drama of that year, yet escaped being totally wrecked by it; and for a more personal reason, because it was the nearest English village to my own home, which is in the forest that surrounded it.

Horstede was on the slopes of a shallow marshy valley. To the north and east, and to the west beyond the valley, it was sheltered by the great forest of Andredeswald, stretching forty miles northward towards the town of London and over a hundred miles from east to west, a natural self-sown forest untouched by man, of native oak, beech, chestnut, ash, birch and holly, and conifers where they were favoured by the soil. To the south from Horstede, down the river valley, the land was more open, and you could see the bare grassy ridge of the chalk hills that run out to the cliffs that are now called Beachy Head. The hills hid the sea, which was twelve miles away as the crow flies.

Horstede is still there, named Little Horsted to distinguish it from another Horsted farther north. Now, a line of electricity pylons marches straight across the ancient village land and the valley; but shutting one's eyes to that, it is still the kind of verdant scene that English exiles dream of. And now on a summer day there is always the distant hum of traffic which is hard to escape in the southern part of England; it is an effort to recall the native silence of the fields and woods, broken only by the hum of bees, the sounds of birds and animals, familiar voices, the wind in the trees, or the almost equally natural sounds of an axe in the forest, or a sickle being sharpened in the fields.

In 1066, between two and three hundred acres had been cleared from the forest by generations of labour, and sixteen men and their families lived there, six cottagers, nine villeins and the thane, whose name was Ulfer. A family could be extensive, with grown-up sons and daughters and their wives and husbands and children, and perhaps some widowed aunts or uncles or orphaned cousins; so there may have been a hundred or even two hundred people in the place. Between them, they had seven and a half ploughs: seven with a team of eight oxen each, and one with a half-team of four. On a stream which ran and still runs along the southern edge of the land, they had a water mill. All of them held their land of Ulfer, and Ulfer as it happened held it directly of King Edward the Confessor, for it was part of a royal hunting estate which extended to the north right through the forest. But Mesewelle, the next village up the river, five miles away, was held in person by Harold Godwineson Earl of Wessex, and the next one down the river, Bercham, was held of the Archbishop of Canterbury.

The cleared land of Horstede, sloping down from the forest edge to the water meadows, looked different then. Now, like most of the south of England, it is a maze of small fields divided by hedges and copses. But then it was farmed as one large open field; and it was ploughed in strips, conventionally ten times as long as they were wide, because of the time and trouble and the wasted headland caused in turning a plough with a team of eight oxen. A standard furrow's length, still called a furlong, was two hundred and twenty yards; the standard width of twenty-two yards, by some mysterious evolution, became the length of a cricket pitch when the game began, not very many years later. These strips of arable land were cropped on a three-year rotation; and although each villein planted and harvested his own crop on the amount of land he held, he might often be allotted different ploughlands. The pasture for sheep and cattle was held in common; perhaps also the herds themselves. So everyone's land, including the thane's, was mixed up together, except the yards and gardens round the houses where each family grew its fruit and vegetables and kept its hens and geese. The annual allotment, like most other things that happened, was decided at village meetings.

As for the houses, they were hardly distinguished from the byres and barns except by the smoke of the fire inside which drifted out through the thatch of the roof. All had wooden frames, hewn of oak or cleft of chestnut, with walls of wattle plastered with clay. A big family had a communal kitchen house where everyone lived round the central fire, and separate sheds for sleeping. The thane's house, Ulfer's, was not much grander than the rest, but it was larger. It had to accommodate anyone who came on lawful business, and indeed the whole community if any danger threatened. To that end, it had a strong palisade, and among the buildings that clustered round it were the priest's house and the church.

The sharing of work in Horstede was more a matter of custom than of law, but an unknown learned person, about the middle of that century, wrote a treatise in Latin on estate management which describes the usual duties of every kind of people from thanes to slaves. It is called *Rectitudines Singularum Personarum*.

There were no slaves in little estates like Horstede. There was a large number in England, but they worked in the households and demesnes of the rich and powerful. The number was falling, partly because the church on the whole encouraged owners of slaves to free them, and partly perhaps because one traditional source of slaves had failed: since time out of mind, prisoners taken in battle had been enslaved, but recently there had been a dearth of battles. Another source was punishment by the courts of law. A man could be enslaved for serious robbery, and so could his family if they were party to the crime, or for persistently failing to pay his taxes or fines: the court condemned him to be sold, and took the profit. There were very few prisons in England then, and probably none where men served long sentences. Enslavement then was the equal of long imprisonment now. No doubt it was more practical, since it made use of a convict's labour and saved the state the expense of keeping him shut up; and one cannot say it was never more merciful. It was also perhaps a final refuge for people too feeble-minded to manage their own affairs.

When slaves were mostly men condemned for crime, it followed that they could only be kept on powerful estates which had a force of soldiery; in a humble place like Horstede, nobody would have wanted them, and nobody could have stopped them running away if they tried and becoming outlaws in the woods. Nevertheless, it was possible to buy a slave in any town, and their value can be guessed from the purchase tax that was paid on such transactions. If a horse was sold, the buyer and seller each paid a penny in tax, and if a man was sold they each paid fourpence.

Slaves therefore had no place in the lives or thoughts of the people of Horstede: they were all free men. The humblest among them were the six cottagers. Some of these may only have been labourers, but among them were probably part-time craftsmen – the miller, a blacksmith, a tinker, foresters, sawyers or hurdle-makers, perhaps a bee-keeper or a potter. To judge by the *Rectitudines*, their cottages were provided by the thane, with up to five acres of the village land and their tools and equipment; and in return they had to work for him one day a week, and three days a week as reapers at harvest time. With few possessions of their own, they were tied to his service; but still, they were free, and if they disliked him enough they could move to another village. They paid no rent, but it was a symbol of their freedom that they paid their dues to the church. That was almost the only thing they needed money for, and their neighbours paid them in kind for the work they did.

The villeins were more substantial people. In the later middle ages, the word villein came to have a servile connotation, but in 1066 these men were the most numerous of heads of families in the countryside, and thought of themselves with pride as being their own masters: the word only came into use about that time, from the Latin villanus, and meant no more than villager. They would have called themselves by the older English title of geburas.

A villein's share of the Horstede land, which he held of the thane, was twenty or thirty acres; and the thane, as a rule, had helped him to start life on his holding by giving him two oxen, a cow, six sheep, seven acres already sown, farm implements and the furniture for his house. These gifts or their equivalent were reclaimed by the thane when the villein died, but normally awarded again to his heir to renew the bargain. In return, the villein owed a formidable list of duties: two days' work a week on the thane's own land, three days' a week at harvest and sowing, the ploughing (shared with the other villeins) of all the thane's arable, seed corn for three acres of it, ten pence a year at Michaelmas, some barley and two hens at Martinmas, either a lamb or two pence at Easter, and a pig for the right to keep his herd in the forest, where they lived on the acorns and beechmast. Perhaps some of these duties were alternatives, but it looks as though the villein needed stalwart sons and daughters to help him, making the holding essentially a family affair. However, he could prosper, feed and clothe the family and keep the fires burning, build up his stock and produce a surplus of wool or hides or cheeses to sell once a year in the town, or to barter, as a communal enterprise, for salt to preserve the winter's meat and iron to make the tools. Salt was brought to Horstede by pedlars from the coast, where there were pans to evaporate sea water; the nearest iron mine recorded in Domesday Book was twelve miles through the forest to the north.

The villeins' and cottars' labour and payments in kind set Ulfer free from working his own landholding, so that he could do the duties of a thane. He paid a hundred shillings a year to the King of whom he held the land, but the King may not have been his immediate lord: Domesday Book recorded that he could take himself where he wished, which is supposed to mean he could give his allegiance to any lord he chose. The most likely were Earl Harold or the Archbishop, who both held manors or villages closer to Horstede than the King's, and so might be better able to offer help and protection in a crisis. The privilege suggests that Horstede was an ancient holding in Ulfer's family, not merely a reward the King had given him.

Whomever he chose as lord, Ulfer was the only man in the village likely to travel far. He had to feed, escort and protect his lord's messengers, probably feed the lord himself and his court for one or more days in the year, look after his hunting rights, build fences and discourage poachers. He had some kind of responsibility for maintaining bridges, and he had to appear and share judgement of crimes and disputes in the hundred court, which met once a month, and perhaps in the shire court which heard more serious cases twice a year.*

* England was divided into earldoms, earldoms into shires and shires into hundreds. Hundreds were so called because they contained, or had once contained, a hundred hides, and a hide was the amount of land that could support a family. But hide and hundred were ancient terms already, and very vague: a hide in Sussex was something about 40 acres, but in East Anglia it was 120. As more land was brought into cultivation, some hundreds came to have far more than a hundred hides, but their

Above all, Ulfer was the man who had to give military service. Thanes, or perhaps their sons or deputies when they grew old, were the mainstay of the fyrd, the army the King could call out, or the earls on the King's behalf, to defend the realm. Each was on call for two months in the year, with his battle-axe sword and mace, his helmet and his coat of chain-mail, or of leather with iron rings sewn on it, and his horse – but a horse for riding only, not for fighting: the English had not trained their horses for battle, but fought on foot. Living within a half-day's ride of the coast, Ulfer would have been called to watch and guard it if ever there was a threat from the English Channel. One way and another, he was often away from home, and then it was probably his wife or son who did his duties in Horstede and kept the village content: he could hardly have been rich enough, with such a small estate, to employ the kind of manager called a reeve.

Horstede was less isolated than many of the villages of England; for one thing, there was another separate and rather smaller village only a mile away on the other side of the millstream. It was called Gorde, and was held by a thane named Helghi. (It is a single farm now, not a village, and its name has evolved to Worth: it has been farmed as a unit for at least a thousand years.) Although Gorde was a separate place, with another thane and another village meeting, and even another mill on the stream, its people were near enough neighbours to make one social community: a young man in Horstede could very easily court a girl in Gorde. And while the forest behind these twin villages was uninhabited, the land to the south, near the coast, was populous. Down there, only twelve miles away by the track beside the valley, was the town of Lewes, which may have had as many as a thousand people, and a manor of the Archbishop which was something of a religious centre. The Roman road from Lewes to London, which carried a good many travellers, passed within a couple of miles of Horstede; but it was on the other side of the river, and to reach it you had to cross by boat, or if you were

boundaries remained the same. The boundaries of the shires were much the same as those of the modern counties.

on horseback go five miles down to Bercham, where there was a ferry, or five miles up, where the river was small enough to ford.

Thus, physically, Horstede people could reach the outside world without much trouble if they wanted to. But isolation, imposed on most villages by distance, was also an attitude of mind. There was no reason for them to go to Lewes, except on an annual expedition to sell the produce they could spare; no reason ever for them to cross the river to the Roman road. No doubt when they did go to town they felt out of place and a little apprehensive, like any country people, and were glad to get home again.

There was one link that joined Horstede to the social system of England, but it was not the town, it was the hundred. Though rule at the top was autocratic, the English of that age were great committee men. Horstede, and any other village, organized its own affairs at a village meeting, a moot, and if they had a problem they could not solve they took it to the hundred moot. Above that was the shire moot, and above all the witena gemot, the embryo parliament which advised the King in his lifetime and appointed his successor when he died.* There was no formal election; the regular members of the higher moots were members *ex officio*, but in theory anyone could attend and speak his mind at any of them, even the witena gemot. In practice, if the village moot could not agree about a problem, it did at least agree in choosing one respected person to put the problem to the hundred moot, where he could discuss it with others from other villages, who could usually think of a precedent and propose an answer.

One senior citizen of Horstede would therefore ride out once a month, perhaps with a solemn and important air, to attend the hundred moot, taking with him Horstede's problem if it had one, and his own wisdom to help to solve the problems of other places in the hundred. But his way was not to town. Horstede's hundred extended in the opposite direction, into the heart of the forest and up the valley, and its moot was held at another village called Flesching, no larger than Horstede itself, in another forest clearing.

* Witan was a plural noun meaning wise men, and witena was its genitive. Hence witena gemot, sometimes written as one word, was a meeting of wise men.

So also was the hundred court that the thane attended. In Flesching, Horstede's emissary would talk with other men who had been as far afield as the shire court, where a bishop or a representative of the earl, or even the earl himself, presided; and when he was seen returning home weary in the evening, one may imagine the other Horstede people converging on his house, and another moot beginning, not only to hear the judgement of the problem but also the gossip of the neighbourhood and the world.

Thus the ten-mile track through the woods to Flesching was Horstede's source of help and justice and news, the tenuous thread that bound the village into the life of England.

The women's view of Horstede is rather more a matter of surmise: not because it was a man's world, but because the writers of the era, who were monks, omitted to write about women. They were far from powerless. A woman could be a landholder: to the east of Horstede along the forest edge, the nearest settlement was a small clearing held of the King by a woman called Aelveva, who seems to have been a freed slave. High up in the social scale, it was common for bridegrooms to give estates to their brides, either as part of a marriage settlement or as the morning gift presented after a satisfactory wedding night – a pleasant custom that has disappeared in England but survives in Scandinavia, where new wives are given morning rings.

But there is an eternal quality in the life of farmers' wives which allows one to make a reliable guess at the way they lived in Horstede; even now, there are wives in the remotest parts of Britain, for example the highlands and islands of Scotland, who do all the things the wives of Horstede must have done, and do them in much the same way. They carded, spun and dyed and wove the wool and made the clothes, boiled the meat and baked the bread, milked the sheep and goats, perhaps the cow, and made the butter and cheese, loved and scolded the children, fed the hens, worked in the fields at harvest, probably made the pots and brewed the beer, and made love or quarrelled with their husbands, or possibly both. And the children, not burdened by school, herded animals, geese or sheep or goats or pigs according to their size. Farmers' wives do not have much material reward, but it would have been a poor farmer in any age who went to town and came home without a fairing. Young men, one presumes, made the journey to buy the pairs of brooches which must have been the most personal possession a woman had and a life-long symbol of an early love; for they were often buried with them.

What else did people do in Horstede, beyond their endless work? There are some clues. Of course they went to church, where the village priest read a simple sermon composed for the purpose by a senior prelate. It is unlikely anyone else in the village could read, except perhaps the thane and his family. But the English were more fortunate than most of the people of northern Europe: the Testament, the lives of saints and many other religious works had been translated from the Latin into the everyday English they spoke. So they could hear them read and understand them.

But they were not particularly solemn people. Not much survives of their sense of humour, but a few riddles that happened to be written down and preserved are healthily bawdy. Certainly they were neither puritan nor prudish; young men and women of course amused each other. Adultery was illegal, and the penalty for rape was castration, but it is hard to imagine the law interfered very much with the love affairs of Horstede.

Out of doors they played some kind of football, and a game with a bat and ball that evolved in later years to the esoteric complexities of cricket. Indoors they played drafts or checkers, and clever people played chess: the kings and queens, bishops, castles and knights must have held for them a topical significance. Perhaps they recognized themselves as pawns. They hunted and fished through necessity, but both have always had an element of sport. The river, now polluted, was teeming with fish, even salmon – water mills commonly paid a tax of hundreds or even thousands of eels – and the forest was full of game; but deer were strictly the King's or earl's prerogative, the penalties for poaching were fearsome, and archery was discouraged among the poor.

They were not merely ignorant yokels. The arts and crafts of

England were known and valued then all over western Europe, especially the illumination of manuscripts, embroidery and gold and silver work; and there was a lively tradition of English prose and verse. Such works of art were mainly creations of the church or the patronage of the rich. But a national reputation usually reflects an inborn national aptitude and taste, and it is safe to assume that village people practised arts of their own and enjoyed the things of beauty they made or saw. Of the materials they could afford, wood, leather, wool or even iron, none was likely to last nine hundred years. The pagan custom of burying treasures with the dead had ended at the coming of Christianity: a woman was buried with nothing but her brooches, and a man with only his knife or hunting spear.

Above all for their amusement, the villagers had an astonishing number of feasts. There were the festivals of the church, and the pagan festivals they had managed to preserve in spite of the church. So there was Christmas and the winter solstice, Easter and May Day, Whitsun, Rogation Day and Lammas, a harvest festival, a sowing festival and a ploughing festival, feasts on appropriate saints' days and feasts on finishing haystacks; not to mention betrothals, weddings and birthdays. They brewed great quantities of beer, and they were uproarious drinkers. One of the principal pleasures of Horstede, after recovering from one festival, must have been looking forward to the next.

Undoubtedly the people of Horstede grumbled too; it has often been observed that whatever rights the English lose, they keep the right to grumble. Yet the *Rectitudines*, and every relevant document of the time, gives a very strong impression of a spirit of give and take, of common sense and kindliness, that the English have not always shown in centuries since. People seem to have been sustained by something that might be called unfashionable now, a positive pleasure in service: they were burdened by the work they did for the thane, but they loved to do it well. They did not resent the grandeur of lords, but enjoyed reflected glory. Earls and their retainers were imperious and formidable men, it was expected of them; but a man might live all his life in Horstede and never see an earl. The thane, in spite of his contacts with the mighty, was very close to the villagers and shared their hopes and disappointments. The grander the lord, the grander was his thane: a King's thane's villein felt himself a cut above the villein of a lesser thane. Horstede, being a fraction of a royal estate, may well have felt honoured, and looked down a little on Mesewelle up the river and Bercham down it, which were held of slightly inferior lords.

This feeling, a good foundation for a stable society, sprang from simple Christianity. The church put pride among the worst of the seven deadly sins, perhaps because its own wealthy prelates were specially tempted by it. The poor were taught and believed that God decreed for every man his station; so envy was subdued. Of course there were cases of cruelty and oppression, but the rich in their better moments acknowledged their wealth and power as gifts of God, to be used in emulation of His justice and mercy. And apparently everyone, rich or poor and saint or sinner, felt a unity in being English, a sense of belonging: a feeling made manifest in the thousands of little places like Horstede by the Englishness of the fields and forest that were home.

In modern terms, it is said a man's happiness largely depends on whether he feels he can understand and control his own environment; and in that respect the people of Horstede were certainly much better off than their industrialized descendants, either in England or elsewhere in the world. They were exposed to droughts and floods, disease and pain; but religion provides a solace for such acts of God. All in all, they had good reason to be happy that New Year's Day, as they recovered from celebrating the birth of Christ and the turning of the winter towards the spring.

But possibly a rumour may have reached them along the forest track from Flesching and cast a small cloud on the feast: the rumour that the King, from whom under God all power flowed, was sick and near his mortal end. If they knew it they would have discussed it, while they downed their Christmas ale, with distant interest and perhaps a hint of foreboding. He had reigned a long time; his strange character, combining kingship with monkish humility, had set a good example; England was used to him. Everyone knew he had no obvious heir: he was too pious, it had always been said, to give his wife a child, and people had made a ribald joke of it. But if he was dying, it was a practical problem. Who would be King? That was something none of them knew, though each of them may have had his theory. Whatever happened, an era was ending, and probably old men of Horstede said gloomily that things would never be quite the same again.

Death of a King

January 4

Most of that New Year's Day the King lay unconscious in an old palace he had rebuilt on Thorney Island, two miles up the river Thames from the city of London. The misty low-lying island, still largely covered by the bramble bushes that gave it its name, with the muddy bank of the tidal river on one side and the marshes of the Tyburn brook on the others, presents a bleak mid-winter scene in contrast to the sheltered homeliness of Horstede; but it had been a place of holy reputation since the earliest days of Christendom in England. Several churches had been founded there and dedicated to St Peter; in the seventh century, the saint was said to have appeared in person to bless the latest building. This was the place the King had chosen for what he considered his life's most important work, the creation of the abbey that came to be known, in distinction from St Paul's cathedral in the city, as the West Minster. He had planned and supervised the work year after year, and while he lay sick the weather vane was mounted on the cupola of the central tower to symbolize completion of the building.

His sickness had started in November. At the time, it was called a malady of the brain; now it might be called a series of cerebral haemorrhages. He seemed to recover from its first onset, but on Christmas Eve he was stricken again. He managed to go through the service and the banquet on Christmas Day, robed and crowned and bearing the regalia. On the next day he could not leave his room. On Wednesday, 28 December, Childermas or Holy Innocents' Day, the great new church was consecrated, but he. could not attend this fulfilment of his life's ambition. Being the man he was, one may be sure he accepted the disappointment as God's rebuke to his pride.

The King's dying was no private agony. The palace must have been crammed with people that Christmas; so must the abbey's monastic buildings and the houses, such as they were, on Thorney Island. The King's own household, his permanent troop of soldiers, the Queen and her attendants, the Benedictine monks of the old foundation and the craftsmen who worked on the building – these were quite enough to fill the place. In addition, a witena gemot had been summoned. Among those present were the two archbishops, of Canterbury and York, eight of the twelve bishops of England, five of the six earls, eight abbots and a crowd of the King's thanes and high officials: in all, at least forty of the greatest men of the kingdom, each with his own retinue.

There was nothing unusual in the summoning of the witan; they always met at Christmas, and the ecclesiastical members at least would certainly have been bidden at any time of the year to such a great event as the consecration. But they had seldom if ever held their mid-winter meeting on that damp constricted island. They had no meeting-place of their own: they met wherever the King happened to be, and for many years he had spent the autumn hunting in the west of England, in Savernake Forest, Cranborne Chase and the Forest of Dean, and had celebrated Christmas at Gloucester. A regular Easter meeting had been held at Winchester, others at Oxford and Canterbury. The King, who held the whole of England, had no one place like a villager that he could call his home.

However, the King's illness probably brought a bigger turn-out than usual, because it brought the witan face to face with a problem that had no precedent. Under the unwritten constitution, it was the duty of the assembly, in the name of the people, not only to advise the King in his lifetime, but to choose his successor when he died. It was not the custom yet, as it was in later ages, for the crown to pass to an heir by formal rules of succession; the time had not come when heralds proclaimed in one breath, 'The King is dead. Long live the King.' The choice was a matter for discussion and if possible unanimous agreement: a huge responsibility, for a king was given great powers for good or evil. In making it, the witan took four things into account. First, a new king should be a man of proper character to rule with strength and justice. Second, he should be of royal blood. Third, he should be English. And fourth, if the dying king was respected, the witan were much inclined to elect an heir he advised. Sometimes, one has to add, they had made a choice that was nothing more than expedient, and elected the man who could back his claim with force.

But King Edward, without any children, had not given them any hint of his wishes, and there was no one man alive who was an obvious choice. There were at least six possibilities. The only living son of the English royal house was Edgar, great-grandson of King Ethelred; but he was only a boy. Of other Englishmen, there were Harold Earl of Wessex and his younger brother Tostig, the deposed and exiled Earl of Northumbria; but they were not of English royal blood. Of foreign kings who might put in a claim, there were Swein of Denmark and Harald Hardrada of Norway; but the witan decidedly did not want a foreigner. And there was Duke William of Normandy, an ambitious man; but not only was he a foreigner – more foreign to the English than the Scandinavian kings – but his hereditary claim was only by marriage: his great-aunt Emma had married two kings of England and was Edward's mother.

So it was not only simple people like the men and women of Horstede who were baffled to know who would be their next anointed king; in Thorney Island too, where the choice soon had to be made, the leaders of the realm were equally at a loss. It is doubtful whether they found much time to mourn for the dying

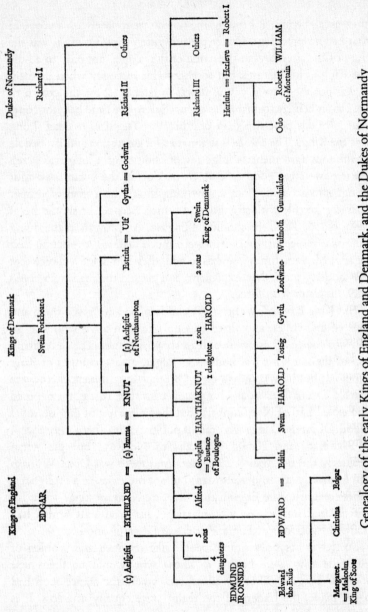

Genealogy of the early Kings of England and Denmark, and the Dukes of Normandy

King: he had not been a bad King, but equally he had not been much of a man to love. In those days of discussion, argument, lobbying, indecision, the only interest of his shuttered apartment was whether he would come to his senses and say whom he wished to succeed him.

The dilemma had its origin exactly fifty years before, and to understand it one has to glance back at political events well known to the witan and within the memory of the older men.

The reign of King Ethelred, who came of the long line of native English kings, had been plagued by Viking raids, and they came to a climax in 1015 when Knut the young son of the King of Denmark invaded England. Soon after, Ethelred died. Some of the witan, meeting at Southampton, accepted Knut as king; others, meeting in London, chose Edmund Ironside, son of Ethelred. War between these rivals, Danish and English, disturbed the country until they agreed to divide it, Knut to reign in the north and Edmund in the south. But six months later, Edmund also died, and the witan then unanimously elected Knut. It was the last time they had given in to force, but Knut turned out to be an effective and beneficent king.

Knut rejected his wife when he came to the throne, and married Emma, the widow of Ethelred – a curious match, because he was only about twenty-one and she was well into her thirties. Ethelred had also been married twice, so that from these two men and their three wives sprang four separate families, seventeen known children altogether. Emma of course remained in England, but the other survivors of the English royal house, including her own children by Ethelred, were sent into exile and scattered over Europe. One of her children was Edward, who was between ten and twelve at the time. He was sent with his younger brother and sister to Normandy, which was Emma's birthplace.

When the foreign invader Knut became king, most eminent Englishmen vanished from history, being executed, banished or imprisoned. But one did the opposite, and suddenly rose into prominence: Godwin. Nobody knows where he came from, and apparently nobody knew at the time. The most circumstantial story is in one of the Scandinavian heroic tales, the Knytlinge Saga: the story that during Knut's invasion a Danish earl named Ulf lost his way and was guided back to his ships by a handsome well-spoken youth whom he found herding cattle, and that Ulf took such a fancy to him that he married him to his sister. The English chroniclers disagree with that story and with each other, but do not put much in its place: one suggests that he was the son of a thane in Sussex, and another that his father was distantly related to a noble house. But not even those who set out to praise him could find a respectable ancestry. Whatever his origin was, Godwin must have been careful to keep it a secret.

One has to admit, perhaps reluctantly, that Godwin was the English genius of the age. His genius was for power – winning, keeping, using and increasing it. Starting from nothing, he became in his early twenties the close companion and adviser of King Knut. He was made an earl, commanded an army for Knut in Denmark, and did in fact marry the sister of Earl Ulf, who was Knut's brother-in-law. Before he was thirty, he was left as the practical ruler of England whenever Knut was abroad. For the rest of his life, which was longer than most, he escaped every kind of danger and remained the most powerful man in the country, not always excepting the king.

Illogical though it may be, the English have usually mistrusted self-made men who win political power for themselves, instead of receiving it as a gift of birth; but Godwin was much more than a power-hungry autocrat. All kinds of Englishmen admired him, especially in his own earldom, which extended right across southern England from Cornwall to Kent. He was said by his friends to be loyal, just and eloquent, he was loved and respected by his family, and although he had jealous enemies they found remarkably little to say against him.

Knut, his first protector, died at the age of forty and was succeeded by two of his sons. The first was Harold, one of the offspring of Knut's first wife – or, as some people said, a changeling, the illicit son of a priest, foisted on Knut by his wife. The second was Harthaknut, a son of Emma. Both were disasters as kings, and both died very young, Harold of mundane disease and Harthaknut, more memorably, through having a fit when he rose to propose the health of the bride and groom at a wedding party.

During Harold's short but awful reign, both the exiles in Normandy ventured back into England, Edward and his younger brother Alfred. Nobody knows what they came for, and Edward got no farther than Southampton. Alfred, with a party of Norman friends, was welcomed by Godwin but then handed over to Harold, who had the friends killed and Alfred so cruelly blinded that he died. Godwin was later tried by the witan for complicity in the crime, and was acquitted. But in the reign of Harthaknut, Edward came back and was received with honour at court.

As a rule, such high political events made little difference in the multitude of humble places like Horstede which were the essence of England. However, one exception was a monstrous new tax imposed by Harthaknut, which was passed on down the ranks of society until the villagers at the bottom had to sell more and eat less of their produce to raise a few more shillings. By the time when he had his welcome fit, English self-respect was ready to revolt against Danish rule; and Godwin, changing with the times, became the champion of rising public opinion. He was the leading spokesman of the witan in 1042 when they chose to defy the Danes and elect an English king again. It had to be Edward. At the age of about thirty-eight, he was the only male survivor of all the seventeen children of Ethelred and Knut. Murder apart, they had been a short-lived brood.

There are several early accounts of the character of Edward and the events of his reign. Reading them, one is brought up at once against the propaganda and the re-writing of history that followed the Norman conquest. The facts of the reign are in the Anglo-Saxon Chronicle; and as it was kept up to date year by year in several monasteries, it reliably represents the opinion of Englishmen at the time. Then there is a biography, *Vita Aedwardi Regis*, written anonymously in Latin by a Flemish monk who lived in England. It was begun not long before Edward died, and was frankly intended to glorify the family of Godwin; but it was finished in very different circumstances after the conquest, when most of the family was dead and praise of it was dangerous. This was the basis of all the later accounts. The Norman ones take an opposite view of Godwin and his sons, twisting the events to make them villains. English accounts written a century later make Edward more of a saint than he seemed to the men who knew him; for by then the English felt nostalgic for the last of their native kings, and the aim of these accounts was to persuade the Pope that he should be canonized. 'Confessor', as he was called in history, was a usual epithet for a saintly person who confessed or avowed his religion in face of danger but did not become a martyr.

But through all the partisanship and special pleading, a surprisingly vivid impression of Edward still survives; he emerges from it all as an individual any reader can recognize. There is no reliable portrait of him, nothing better than the heads on his coins and the conventional sketches of the Bayeux tapestry and the later documents. All they can really be said to have in common is a beard, which was not the highest of fashion in England then. Yet somehow, taken together, they seem to show a long, thin and rather lugubrious face, which is just what one would expect; for he had grown up to be a melancholy man, as if he had never recovered from the shock of his exile as a child. To lose his father, to be rejected by his mother so that she could marry his father's mortal enemy, and then to be abandoned to foreign-speaking cousins in an alien land – this was a cruel experience for a boy of ten or twelve, and quite enough to account for the oddity of his character as a man. He bore a grudge against his mother for thirty years, and when he had the power he deprived her of all the wealth she had amassed – but characteristically he repented soon afterwards and gave it all back again. He did not marry until he was over forty, when it became a political obligation, and he had no other recorded relationship with a woman. Homosexuality was common enough to be recognized and accepted in those days, and given the behaviour of Edward's mother a psychiatrist would not be surprised to find a homosexual son; but to judge by his reputation, whatever instinct he had was strictly repressed. His marriage lasted with one political lapse until he died, and at the end he spoke of his wife as a 'beloved daughter'. Its fatal barrenness may have had physical causes either in him or his wife that nobody understood; if he refused to consummate it, as people believed, distaste and inhibition are likelier reasons than piety. After all, it was not and never had been an impious act. But one can imagine a man distressed and embarrassed to find he could not manage it, and persuading himself – and trying to persuade his wife, who was only half his age – that chastity even in marriage was a virtue. His most perceptive modern biographer has said that 'he always behaved like one who has been deprived of love.'

Pious he certainly was, even priggish in the eyes of his robuster followers. No doubt he had turned to religion for comfort in his lonely youth: as a man, he saw the hand of God or the devil in every event, and divided most of his time between religious observances and hunting. Even on his long expeditions in the forests he caused mass to be said before the day's slaughter began. 'After divine service', the *Vita* says, 'which he gladly and devoutly attended every day, he took much pleasure in hawks and birds of that kind which were brought before him, and was really delighted by the baying and scrambling of the hounds.' His piety, looking back on it now, seems rather too ostentatious, and a hunting saint seems anomalous; yet in his lifetime he had something of a reputation for prophetic dreams and miraculous cures of the sick and blind, and more miracles were recorded years after his death when his canonization was in question. It must be said for him that he never went out of his way to claim miraculous powers, though he was not displeased when he heard of a cure that worked. Some of the cures were achieved by drinking the water he had washed in, or sprinkling it on the eyes of the blind, and sometimes his servants preserved the wonderful bath-water and administered it, perhaps for a fee, without telling him.

Almost everything he did as king was done in prayer and long examination of his conscience. The exceptions were the things he did when he lost his temper. In a rage, he was almost out of his mind and was ruthless with anyone who offended him, though never physically cruel: he did not kill, imprison or mutilate his political enemies, he punished them with exile like his own. But when his anger cooled, he was penitent, prayed for forgiveness, forgave the offenders and often invited them home again. That was certainly virtuous, but not a good basis for a consistent royal policy. To salve his own conscience, he let some dangerous men go free.

A second natural result of his exile was that he grew up more Norman than English in his tastes and manners. He was educated by Norman priests and trained in the martial sports by Norman knights. When he came back to England he spoke Norman French more often than English, and most of his friends were Norman. Some followed him, and he clung to them with a rather pathetic fidelity, as if without them the return to England would have seemed a second exile. There were not a great many of them, but their presence close to the King was a constant annoyance to the English who happened to meet them: especially to the most English of Englishmen, Earl Godwin.

For Godwin, the choice of Edward as king had special advantages, apart from his English descent. There was only one limit to Godwin's ambition: with his mysteriously humble birth he could not hope to be chosen king himself. He could only be a power behind the throne. On the other hand, he had six sons and at least one beautiful talented daughter. Edward looked like a weak-willed man who might be expected to do as he was told. Moreover, he was a bachelor. So it seemed possible that every earl of England might be a Godwin, the queen might be a Godwin, the next king of England Godwin's grandson and he himself the co-founder of a dynasty.

Within three years of Edward's accession, Godwin was well on the way to achieving this unique position. His two eldest sons Svein and Harold were earls, meekly created by Edward, and his nephew Beorn was another. Four of the six great earldoms were held by the family, two-thirds of England were under its rule, and four more sons were growing up and waiting for promotion. The family's income from its vast estates was equal to the King's. And it was Godwin's daughter Edith that Edward agreed to marry.

But no two men could have been less alike: Edward conscience-ridden, introspective, selfish, impractical and puritan – Godwin hearty, pragmatic, extrovert, a man who enjoyed his food and drink and other animal comforts and seemed to care less about his soul's salvation, the only rich man of his time who never bothered to found a church or endow an abbey to absolve his sins. No wonder they always seem to have disliked each other. Edward was clearly afraid of Godwin, yet was too weak to rule without him. He must have come to feel he was surrounded by Godwins: four of them in his immediate council, one in his bed and several more, teenagers and children, hanging round his palaces and waiting expectantly for honours. He developed an obstinate unpredictable will of his own, and could not resist annoying Godwin with spiteful and trivial objections to the policies he proposed – objections he could always support by claiming a better knowledge of God's will. Probably he annoyed him most of all by his futile performance as a husband.

It says a lot for Godwin's patience and loyalty that the two of them kept England peaceful and prosperous for the first ten years of the reign. But his ambition was thwarted and his pride was perhaps subdued by the bad behaviour of his eldest son Svein. Svein was the black sheep of the family. When he was twenty-four he seduced an abbess, a very unusual sin. Edward sent him into exile, then forgave him and let him come home: but next he murdered his cousin Beorn. He was exiled again and forgiven again, but this time on condition that he made a penitential pilgrimage to Jerusalem. He is said to have walked there barefooted, and on the way back he died in Constantinople. So Harold, the second son, was left as Godwin's heir.

In 1048, Edward and Godwin quarrelled. It was the climax of years of vexation: the immediate cause was the King's un-English respect for his foreign favourites. A Frenchman called Count Eustace of Boulogne, who had married Edward's sister (it was a second marriage for both) came over to visit the King. On their way home, this outlandish count and his followers rode into the town of Dover armed and armoured and demanded accommodation. One householder refused to admit an armed foreigner into his home, the foreigner attacked and wounded him, and the householder killed the intruder. The fracas spread until twenty burghers of Dover were dead and nineteen foreigners, and the count rode back to the King in a rage to demand revenge. Edward was also enraged at the insult to his guest, and was further incited by his Norman friends, especially one named Robert whom he had appointed Archbishop of Canterbury. He sent for Godwin and told him to punish the town, which was in his earldom. Godwin refused, because the case of the people of Dover had not been heard. That made Edward even more uncontrollably furious, and he accused Godwin again of the crime of which he had already been acquitted, the murder of Edward's brother Alfred twelve years before.

England came close to civil war over this affair, with rival armies, Godwin's and the King's, confronting each other across the Thames at London. It was a trial of wills between the King's English and foreign advisers. War was averted by the native common sense of the people, and of the earls who were not directly involved: they said they would not fight other Englishmen because it would lay the country open to foreign invaders. In the upshot, Dover was not punished, but Godwin and all his sons were given five days to leave the country. Edward, furious with the whole family, even deprived his own wife of all she possessed and sent her to a nunnery. For the moment, his foreign friends had won control of him and he resigned himself entirely to their advice.

Edward ought to have known he had gone too far, and if he had not been so angry he would have known it. The behaviour of Eustace had outraged all the Englishmen who heard of it and roused the stubborn insularity they can still show today: to put it in the terms they might use now, these damned foreigners, counts or whatever they called themselves, could do what they liked at home, but if they wanted to come to England they had better learn how to behave. Edward had put himself hopelessly in the wrong. To pacify the detestable count, he had tried to deny two rights his own people were ready to insist on, the right to possess their homes in peace and the right to defence at law.

The next year, Godwin came back without the King's permission and landed in the Isle of Wight. He sailed along the shore of his earldom, greeted as a hero, collecting more ships and men in all the harbours, Pevensey, Hastings, Romney, Hythe, Sandwich and Dover itself. The King sent ships to find him, but they failed and retired to London. Godwin came after them. Below London Bridge he anchored to wait for the tide, and when it turned he lowered his masts and his fleet drifted under the arches. The King's fleet was drawn up on the north bank between London and Thorney Island, and Godwin anchored again along the south bank, which had been the border of his earldom. The trial of wills began again. Godwin sent messengers to the King, not threatening him but declaring his loyalty and craving the return of the earldoms that had been taken from him and Harold. The King refused. Godwin's men urged him to fight it out. But the witan, led by Stigand, Bishop of Winchester, crossed the river to argue a peaceful settlement. The King's French friends, seeing public opinion against them, lost their nerve and fled from the town: the French archbishop fought his way out at Eastgate and escaped up the Essex coast, where he 'lighted on a crazy ship' and vanished back to France.

Deserted, Edward had to give in. A gemot was assembled and Godwin made a speech, declaring 'before King Edward his lord and before all the people of the country' that he and his children were innocent; and the King, with bad grace, reinstated Godwin and Harold, pardoned their followers and brought back his Queen from the nunnery. The witan shrewdly put all the blame on the King's French advisers for causing discord among the English, and many of them were outlawed. Stigand, who had made the peace, was appointed archbishop in place of the runaway Frenchman.

It had all been a storm in a teacup, but in the light of later events the affair had special significance. It showed the strength in that era of English institutions. Nobody, not even the King, was above the law. The humble householders of Dover had rights that could not be denied. The witan were indeed wise men, who could hold the peace when the two strongest men in the country were poised for civil war. It even proved the strength of the monarchy: the King's was a sacred office, blessed by God, and even when he affronted his people and his most powerful earl, they treated him with deference. And it proved that England was English, and that Englishmen who had freed themselves from the Danes were not in a mood to tolerate foreign interference.

There were two other omens in the quarrel. One was that Count Eustace and his men had mounted their horses to fight the people of Dover: the first time Englishmen had encountered men who fought on horseback. The other was that while Godwin was in exile and the French had the influence at court, Duke William of Normandy came in state to visit King Edward, and had long and private conversations with him.

A year after his exile, at Easter 1053, Godwin died. The accounts of his death provide an example of Norman propaganda. The English account in the Anglo-Saxon Chronicle, written within a year of the event, is a clinical description of a cerebral haemorrhage: 'On the second day of Easter (at Winchester) he was sitting at dinner with the King, when he suddenly sank down by the footstool, deprived of speech and of all his strength. He was taken into the King's chamber, and it was thought the attack would pass over. But it did not; he continued, speechless and powerless, until the Thursday, and then resigned his life.'

The Norman version, written down eighty years later in a biographical poem called *La Estoire de Seint Aedward le Rei*, made Godwin's death a final proof of his wickedness: for the Normans tried to justify their attack on England by the story that Godwin and all his sons were villains who had victimized the saintly king. In this version, a servant bringing wine at dinner slipped on the steps of the dais with one foot and saved himself with the other. Godwin made a joke: 'So one brother helps the other when he is in danger.' 'So might my brother have helped me,' the King said, 'if you, Earl, had let him live.' At this the earl changed colour (as well he might, for he had twice been acquitted of complicity in that ancient crime, by the highest court in the land and by the King himself). But he proposed a trial:

'Now he takes a piece of bread and holds it up,
And says, "If I can enjoy
This morsel which you see me hold,
Which I will eat in the sight of you all,
Then all at the table will see
That I am not to blame for this death;
So I am either acquitted or found guilty."
King Edward blesses the morsel,
And says, "May God grant that the proof be true."
The earl puts it in his mouth,
The morsel is fixed like a stick
In the opening of the throat
Of the traitorous felon glutton,
So that all the table can see it.
His eyes roll back in his head,
His flesh blackens and becomes pale.
All are astonished in the hall:
He loses breath and speech
From the morsel which sticks fast.
Dead is the bloody felon;
Much power had the blessing
Which gave virtue to the morsel;
At last was the murder proved.
"Now," cries the King,
"Drag out this stinking dog." '

The story is not incredible in itself. Trial by ordeal was part of the judicial system then, and everyone believed it revealed a heavenly judgement of guilt or innocence. If Godwin had had a guilty conscience he might have found it hard to swallow the bread, especially after Edward's sanctimonious blessing. One can even believe that Edward might still have harboured his secret suspicion: he was a vindictive, irrational man.

But it is incredible that such a dramatic event could have been hushed up at the time and never become common knowledge in England or found its way into English chronicles. And Edward's behaviour afterwards could not possibly have followed such a revelation of Godwin's guilt, for all the honours of Godwin passed to his family. Edith remained Queen, and Edward seems to have loved her in his peculiar way. Harold was promoted to his father's earldom and became the King's right hand, and as other earldoms fell vacant three of the four remaining sons were created earl, Tostig, Gyrth and Leofwine. (The only one who was not ennobled was the youngest, Wulfnoth, who had been given, presumably by Edward, as a hostage to Duke William, and remained imprisoned in Normandy for over thirty years till the Duke died in 1087.)

So after Godwin's death his family remained as highly regarded as ever, both by the King and by the English people. The Norman story can only be a political myth. But it is tempting to believe a part of it: that the servant did trip on the steps, that Godwin did make the feeble joke, that the King did express his fantastic suspicion – and that Godwin's indignation at being accused again after so many years of patient loyalty sent his blood pressure up and caused a haemorrhage that killed him.

About the time of Godwin's death, people began to worry about the succession to the throne. By then, nobody could have hoped that Edward and Edith would produce an heir, and nobody seems to have thought of Edith's brothers, Godwin's sons, as possible candidates. So the Bishop of Worcester was sent abroad in 1054 to find survivors of the royal house who had been scattered in exile when Knut was crowned. The only one still alive turned out to be another Edward, known as the Exile, who was the son of King Edmund Ironside. Knut had sent him as an infant to the King of Sweden with the understanding that he would be quietly killed, but the King of Sweden had sent him on to the King of Hungary; and there, far away, he had grown up, and married and had two daughters and a son. He must have been entirely Hungarian in his view of life, but he gave his children Norse or English names, Margaret, Christina and Edgar.

It took three years of search and persuasion, but in 1057 this unlucky man had been found and was brought back to England;

where, soon after he landed and before he had a chance to meet the King, he died. The King took the children into his household, and it was said he brought them up as if they had been his own. Perhaps, if he thought about it at all, it was the little boy Edgar, who was five, whom he regarded as his natural heir, but the only thing he seems to have said about the succession was that God would provide. It may have been a sincere belief, and it was also a good way of keeping people guessing.

In that second half of Edward's reign, England remained a calm and peaceful place, where men and women were free to occupy their minds with eternally important matters like weather and crops. The monks who compiled the Anglo-Saxon Chronicle found nothing more to record than the deaths of their bishops and an occasional foray across the borders, led by the earls, to subdue the passions of the Welsh and Scots – this was the lifetime of Macbeth. Edward still had some French friends, but they took no obvious part in politics, and his own part became more whimsical and inter-mittant. Most of the time he was happy to leave the secular govern-ment to the earls, and above all to Harold. Harold, in those years, was the factual ruler of the country. It was a status no Englishman had ever had before, and new titles began to appear in documents. He was described as Dux Anglorum, leader or Duke of the English, or as Subregulus, Under-King. Sometimes, even more royally, it was Dei Gratia Dux: nobody but a King before had been said to hold power by the Grace of God. Yet he served his eccentric master as loyally as his father had before him, and with less apparent exasperation. The peace of England was mostly of Harold's making, and the English knew it was.

The most momentous event of those years had occurred only three months before the witan met at the deathbed of the King. At that mid-winter meeting on Thorney Island they were still suffering from the shock of it, and indeed the shock may have been the cause of Edward's fatal sickness. For among those present were three of the noble sons of Godwin, Harold, Gyrth and Leofwine, but not the fourth: Tostig had been exiled.

In September that year, 1065, Tostig had been hunting with the

King on his autumn expedition in the western forests when news was urgently brought that his earldom of Northumbria was in revolt and an army of its people was marching south. They were led by his thanes, and had killed his armed retainers in his capital of York, plundered his treasury and armoury and declared him an outlaw. They demanded that Edward should dismiss him and give them another earl, a boy named Morkere, the younger brother of the Earl of Mercia – who himself was a teenager.

There is some evidence in the *Vita Aedwardi Regis* that Tostig had always been Edward's favourite among the Godwins. He was a boy of about fifteen when Edward came to the throne; Edward had seen him grow up, and was certainly capable of real affection for younger men. At the news from the north, his first angry reaction was to use all his power in support of Tostig, to call up his armies and put down the rebels by force. But most of his advisers were against it, saying Tostig must be to blame: a popular revolt against an earl was unthinkable if the earl had governed justly. Tostig, in what seems a desperate bid to defend himself, accused his brother Harold of stirring up the trouble. Harold swore a solemn oath that he had not. Whatever the King believed, Harold was the only man he had with authority to mediate, and he sent him to meet the rebels at Northampton taking an ultimatum: they must first lay down their arms, and then the King would hear their complaints.

Harold came back with a tragic personal dilemma. The rebels had convinced him they would never have his brother back, whatever the King said or did, and that their complaints were true: Tostig had despoiled their churches, taxed them unjustly and twisted the law to rob and murder his enemies. And they had given a counter-ultimatum: the King must dismiss Tostig, or they would attack the King himself. To give point to the threat, they marched farther south to Oxford.

That made Edward even angrier, and he summoned his army to mobilize. But none of his troops arrived: his orders were simply disobeyed. Tostig claimed that Harold had a grudge against him and wanted to get rid of him. The only reason ever suggested is that Harold might have wanted the throne and suspected Edward

meant to nominate Tostig as his heir. But there is not the faintest
evidence of it. On the contrary, the whole affair, the refusal to obey
the furious King, seems another example of the innate wisdom of
the English people, and this time of Harold as a leader. For the past
generation, England had been governed by consent. All the power
the King could muster was not enough to govern by force and fear.
Nothing justified civil war. It was far better that Tostig should
suffer than that hundreds or thousands of humbler men should
suffer for him.

By leading this opinion, Harold made his brother an implacable
enemy. The King raged, but there was nothing he could do. He had
to submit, send Tostig abroad and give the rebels the earl they
wanted: and it was in his rage that he had the first of his seizures.

Here then were all the origins of the witan's dilemma when they
met that drear mid-winter in the knowledge that the King was
dying: here also the reasons why they waited so anxiously hoping
that in a moment of consciousness he would tell them his choice as
heir. His choice was not binding, the decision was theirs. But with
so little to guide them, a single word from him was likely to be
decisive. What was more, the future king, whoever he was, would
be strengthened against the rival claimants by the old King's blessing.

Would he name the boy Edgar, the only male survivor of the
royal house? If so, could a boy of thirteen hold the country against
the rivals? Would it be Harold, who had carried most of the burden
of government for the past ten years? Would the King revert to his
love of Tostig in spite of Tostig's indelible disgrace? Had he made
any promise in the past, perhaps to one of the Scandinavian kings,
or, most unwelcome of all, to his Norman friends in the old days?
What had he said to Duke William fifteen years before, in that brief
time when the Godwins were in eclipse and the Normans in the
ascendant? Did he expect some miraculous revelation after his
death of the will of God for England?

The author of the *Vita*, knowing the importance of the deathbed
scene, has left a very detailed account of it. It is unlikely he was in
the King's bedroom himself, but he must have heard first-hand

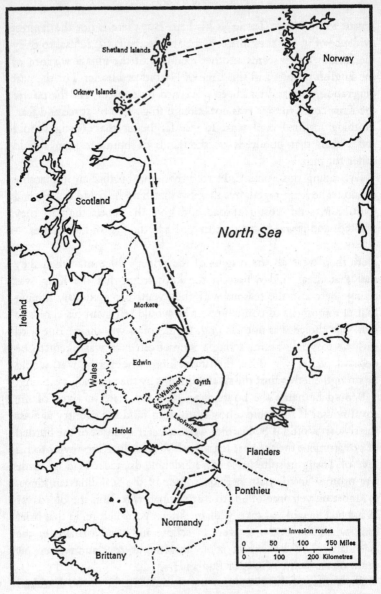

The earldoms of England in 1066
and the invasion routes

accounts from people who were, especially from the Queen, for it was she who commissioned him to write the King's biography.

Four people were constantly present: others came and went. There was the Queen: she is portrayed in the Bayeux tapestry at the foot of the bed, trying to warm her husband's feet in her lap. There was Harold, as senior earl of England and the King's closest adviser. The Archbishop of Canterbury was there as priest, the same Stigand who had wisely settled the quarrel between the King and Godwin. And there was one of the King's remaining foreign friends, Robert FitzWimark, who was part Breton and part Norman. His only qualification was friendship, but it was important, as things turned out, that there was a foreign witness of the scene. Nothing would have suited the Normans better, in the next few months, than to deny what happened on this all-important occasion, but they never did. Robert FitzWimark must have given the same report as everybody else.

In the first days of the New Year, the King's coma or sleep was interrupted by periods of delirium, and on 4 January he was distressingly restless, though still unconscious. They tried to rouse him from this uneasy sleep, and succeeded. When he awoke, he asked them to assemble his household and a few more people came into the room: we are not told who they were. Then he began to speak in a strong voice. But instead of telling them what they needed to know, he gave them a long account of a dream. He had met two monks he had known in Normandy, who were long since dead. They had told him that for the wickedness of the earls and churchmen of England God had cursed the country: a year and a day after his death, devils would come through the land with fire and sword and war. God would only cease to punish England when a green tree, felled half-way up its trunk and the part cut off taken three furlongs away, should join itself together again by its own efforts, without the aid of man, and break into leaf and fruit again.

With Edward's prophetic reputation, this dream was remembered and interpreted long afterwards. For the moment, it alarmed the listeners but annoyed the archbishop, who whispered to Harold that the King was old and sick and raving. But then he seemed to collect himself and spoke his final will. 'Do not mourn for me,' he said, 'but pray to God for my soul and give me leave to go to him. He who allowed himself to die will not allow me not to die.'

To comfort the Queen, who was weeping, he said she was not to fear, for by God's mercy he would not die then but would become well again: she understood him to mean that he was passing to eternal life. And in everyone's hearing he prayed, 'May God reward my wife for her devoted loving service. For she has been a devoted servant to me, always at my side like a beloved daughter.'

Then he offered his hand to Harold with the words that everyone awaited. 'I commend this woman and all the kingdom to your protection,' he said. 'Serve and honour her with faithful obedience as your lady and sister, which she is, and do not deprive her, as long as she lives, of any honour she has received from me. I also commend to you those men who have left their native land for love of me and served me faithfully. Take an oath of fealty from them if they wish, and protect and retain them; or send them with your safe conduct across the Channel to their own homes with all they have acquired in my service.'

Then he gave to Harold instructions for his burial in the new minster and asked him not to conceal the death but announce it promptly everywhere, so that all the faithful could ask the mercy of God on him, a sinner.

Afterwards the King fell back into a coma. The last rites were administered, and on 4 or 5 January, probably in the night between, he died.

Coronation

January 5

On first thoughts it is strange that the scene reported by the author of the *Vita* is not more specific. He was frankly a supporter of the Godwin family, but he did not claim that the King said clearly in so many words that Harold was his chosen heir. On the face of it, Edward's words are equivocal. In commending the Queen, the country and his servants to Harold's protection, he might simply have been assuming that Harold would be King, perhaps having even forgotten in his dying state that he had not said so before, or that there could be any question about it. Or he could have been assuming the opposite: that Harold would carry on, as he had for so many years, as the effective governor of the country, the loyal servant of the crown, and that somebody else would arrive to be anointed king – somebody who was not present, somebody perhaps with a prior claim, or somebody chosen by God's direct inter-vention. There may have been a precedent for this kind of inter-regnum: one chronicle, the Winchester Annals, says Godwin acted as a regent between the death of Harthaknut and the coronation of Edward.

Perhaps the report contains the words of the King as exactly as anyone present could remember them: the author seems a careful historian who did his best to be right in matters of fact. But if it is deliberately vague, there is a ready explanation: this part of the *Vita* was written very soon after the Norman conquest when overt supporters of Harold were being ruthlessly repressed. At that time, it would have been more than the author's freedom was worth to assert that Harold was Edward's chosen heir, and so to imply that the Norman invasion was utterly unjust. He may have gone as far as he dared, and to dare so much he must have been perfectly certain in his own mind of what the King intended.

But any lingering doubt arises only from the written report. The salient fact is that the dying words of the King left no doubt whatever in the minds of the people who heard them, or those who heard them repeated, as they instantly were, among the throng on Thorney Island. There was no more discussion: the King had named Harold; the very same day, the witan confirmed the choice. Some of them may have hesitated before about the propriety of appointing a King who, although he was brother of the Queen, was not of royal birth; but now the choice had been blessed by the last of the hereditary kings.

It was what they wanted to hear: it simplified things. Harold had all the other qualities they looked for. He was English, they all knew him, he had governed for years with justice, he had no notable English enemies except his brother Tostig who had gone, he cared much more for the church than his father had, and he was a soldier. There is no suggestion in any chronicle that the choice was not unanimous: nobody, not even the remaining Normans, fell from power by opposing it, as Englishmen fell from power at the choice of Knut or Danes at the choice of Edward.

When the news went round a few hours later that the King was dead, the predominant feeling was probably still relief that the witan's problem had been settled in time.

To make a portrait of Harold, one first ought to look at the aristocratic society he lived in – the opposite end of the social scale from

Horstede. The life of the gentry is harder to describe than the life of the peasants. The monastic chroniclers were not sympathetic to wealth, except when it was given as offerings to the church or alms to the poor; and moreover they were writing after the downfall of this aristocracy, and had to search for wickedness among the men of power which would account for the wrath of God against them.

It was certainly not a lazy life, or even comfortable. Lords had to travel, to follow the king around, attend the meetings of the witan and administer their own domains; and when they were not doing that, their favourite occupation was hunting. So they spent most of their days on horseback, summer and winter. At home they lived in houses that were bigger than the villagers' but not much more ornate, and probably colder and draughtier; for without window glass and without any heat but a log fire, the only way to keep snug in winter, one would imagine, was to live in a very small cottage. Nor were there many luxuries money could buy. The rich had more food, more drink, and more elegant clothes, but not much more variety. They depended like everyone else on the native products of England – bread, meat, butter and eggs, dried fish in Lent and on Fridays, nothing sweet except honey and the local fruit when it was ripe. Once in a while, perhaps, they acquired a bale of silk or some spices, cloves or pepper, brought at enormous cost along the ancient roads of Asia and through the length of Europe. The greatest pleasure of wealth was simply the exercise of power, for better or worse: to have the choice of being generous or stern.

But things were changing. The second generation of Godwins was not so insular as the old man, and under its influence Edward's court became almost cosmopolitan. There were people in it with English, Norman, French, Flemish and Scandinavian names, and apparently racial friction was forgotten; and there were often delegations from abroad. It also became more up-to-date in its fashions. Edward affected not to care about clothes: he was reluctant to wear 'the regal finery in which the Queen obligingly arrayed him', and said it was too expensive – though sometimes he did remember to thank her. But his puritan foreign guests, in the later years of his reign, were shocked by the elegance and the long fair hair of the younger men, and by boys who were as beautiful as girls, and they concluded like many visitors since that the English were decadent.

The monks thought so too. William of Malmesbury wrote an inventory of the sins of the nobility which he believed had led to their downfall. It does not seem a very wicked list. 'Given up to luxury and wantonness,' he says, 'they did not go to church in the morning as Christians should, but merely, in a careless manner, heard matins and masses from a hurrying priest in their chambers, among the blandishments of their wives. Drinking in parties was a universal practice, in which they passed entire nights as well as days. They consumed their whole substance in mean and despicable houses, unlike the Normans and French who in noble and splendid mansions lived with frugality. They used to eat till they were sur-feited and drink till they were sick. One of their customs, repugnant to nature, was to sell their female servants, when pregnant by them and after they had satisfied their lust, either to public prostitution or foreign slavery. They wore gold bracelets, and short garments down to the knee, shaved their beards and had their skin tattooed.' Even he admits there were exceptions, and one cannot help feeling that most aristocracies would have come off worse at the hands of a critical monk. Apart from the fate of the female servants, it sounds an easy-going, cheerful and fairly harmless life.

To discover what sort of man Harold was, one has to separate Norman and English opinion and steer a course between them; for Harold became the main target of the Normans' self-justification, and their slanders were so outrageous that the same English monks were goaded to defend him with exaggerated praise. Six years after the conquest, to take one Norman example, Duke William's chaplain, William of Poitiers, wrote a work in praise of his master in which he addressed the English: 'If only you would cast aside your foolishness and wickedness you would love . . . the man who now has power over you; for he removed from your neck the proud and cruel despotism of Harold, and killed the hateful tyrant who had reduced you to ruinous and shameful slavery.' But that was not how the English remembered Harold, as this Norman writer acknowledged. Indeed it was nonsense: the Normans often damaged their case by overstating it. Harold, whatever else, was not a cruel despot or a hateful tyrant, and the English, as the Duke discovered, were not very easy to reduce to shameful slavery.

Against this kind of calumny, Florence of Worcester, writing early in the following century, went as far in the opposite direction. After the coronation, he said, Harold 'began to abolish unrighteous laws, to establish righteous ones, to be the patron of churches and monasteries, to reverence bishops, abbots, monks and churchmen of every sort, to show himself pious, lowly and affable to all good men, and to be the enemy of evil doers.'

To find the middle course between the two extremes, one has to rely rather heavily on the author of the *Vita Aedwardi Regis*, but that is not unreasonable – he wrote this part of the story before the Norman attacks began, and he was the only historian who knew Harold personally. He admired him, but not uncritically. He described the characters of Harold and Tostig together and succeeded most ingeniously in disguising his criticism of either of the brothers as praise of the other. So he left a dual character sketch which has the ring of truth and is often corroborated by events.

Harold, then, was in his early forties when he was chosen King, tall, handsome enough, healthy and strong except for attacks of what might have been rheumatism, and a courteous cheerful companion. He was patient, and kind to men of good will, 'but disturbers of the peace, thieves and robbers, this champion of the law threatened with the terrible face of a lion.' Tostig was sometimes over-zealous in attacking evil, but Harold was even-tempered and sympathetic. He shared his plans with anyone he thought was loyal, and had a quality rare in men of power in any age: he could bear contradiction well, and never retaliated for it. 'Both persevered with what they had begun; but Tostig vigorously, Harold prudently; in action the one aimed at success, the other also at happiness. Both at times so cleverly disguised their intentions that one who did not know them was in doubt what to think.'

As for their private lives, Tostig renounced desire for all women except his wife of royal stock (she was Flemish); and here, by one of his significant omissions, the monkish author implies that Harold was more liberal in his loves. In fact there was a lady named Edith Svanneshals, which means Swan's Throat, who was constant enough to have borne him three sons and may have been his lover for twenty years, but never held the rank of an earl's official wife. Perhaps there had not been much time in his life for domesticity: besides governing his own enormous earldom, he had always been at Edward's bidding, ready to ride at a moment's notice the length of the kingdom, to fight the King's battles in Wales or, more often, to soothe the feelings of men the King had offended. The King's service had made him 'well practised in endless fatigues and in doing without sleep or food.' He had a reputation of marching faster and farther than anyone else thought possible.

Godwin, Harold's father, had no pretensions to learning, but with his high ambitions he saw to the education of his children in the scholarly subjects of the age – history, religion, languages and arts. Cultured Englishmen or women had to be linguists then: they could not expect anyone else to speak English. Edith, Harold and Tostig understood French, probably Norse and Flemish, and possibly Latin. Edith would seem to have been more scholarly than Harold, and Harold more than Tostig. But Harold grew up with at least a respect for learning: the abbey he founded and endowed at Waltham in Essex was not a monastic establishment but a secular college. (It also enshrined the Holy Rood, a miraculous stone crucifix of mysterious origin.) All his life, he went on teaching himself, especially in the art of government. Both the brothers made journeys abroad, including the pilgrimage to Rome. Tostig is praised in the *Vita* for his devotions at all the shrines of saints along the way: Harold is not. But Harold made use of the journey to study the policies, characters and strength of the princes of other countries, and is said to have learned so much about them that he could not be deceived by any of their proposals. The pilgrimage was perilous and beset by brigands. Tostig's party was waylaid and plundered, 'some even to nakedness', within a day's march of Rome, and Tostig only escaped because a young companion pretended to be the earl and let himself be captured. Harold did better. The author, in one of his telling phrases, says that 'by God's grace he came home, passing with watchful mockery through all ambushes, as was his way.'

Harold has had the misfortune in history to be remembered for what his foreign enemies said of him, more than for what his friends and subjects said; because after the conquest Norman voices were strident and Englishmen subdued. But the Normans' verbal attacks were made quite openly to justify themselves by discrediting him; they were the kind of political propaganda, familiar today, which even the propagandists know is untrue. The *Vita*, and all the other scattered opinions of Englishmen who knew him, and his own actions, leave an absolutely different impression of Harold which one can only think is much closer to the truth: the impression of a very capable man, patient, friendly, tolerant, good humoured and easy-going by nature – but a man who knew his own mind and could be tough if he had to.

He can hardly be called a genius and nobody ever claimed he was a saint – though one of his long-standing friends was Wulfstan, the sainted Bishop of Worcester. Compared with Edward, he was refreshingly normal. He was approachable, a man who would listen to complaints and other people's troubles, and understand and exchange the jokes of his soldiers. He had the charm to cool the impatience or anger of other people and soothe their injured pride. He preferred to persuade men to agree rather than fight them if they disagreed, aiming, as the author of the *Vita* put it, not only at success but happiness: all the coins minted in his reign bore the one word PAX. And if this impression seems partisan, it is confirmed by his years as Subregulus, as second-in-command to Edward. Edward's whims and rages and sanctimonious manner must have been a daily test of anybody's patience, and often have given Harold the job of apologizing for the King's decisions or persuading him to change them. Godwin had done it too; but Godwin had made his reputation long before Edward came to the throne, and was already regarded then as a father-figure. Harold had to begin to do it when he was under thirty. Yet he succeeded, all those years, in keeping England at peace and remaining the trusted friend of the wayward King;

and he did it without making any Englishman his mortal enemy except, in the end, his own brother. It was a great achievement.

One wonders whether he hoped to be king himself: it must often have seemed an easier job than the one he had. Historians have assumed he wanted to be, but for no better reason than that normal men are always assumed to be ambitious: he never showed he wanted it by any act that was reliably reported. Eight years before, when Edward the Exile was brought back from Hungary, Harold could only have expected to serve this second Edward as he served the first. When the Exile died, there was his son, the boy Edgar. If the King had lived another couple of years, Edgar would have been fifteen and certainly considered old enough to reign. One cannot imagine Harold would rashly have tried to oppose him, if only because he might easily have failed. So whatever he hoped, it can only have been in the last few weeks or even days, when the King was seen to be dying, that Harold had any positive expectation of being anointed. Yet in everything that can be known about him, he seems to have been typical of the Englishmen of his time, and to have had the makings of an honest king.

Edward was buried in his abbey the morning after he died, and the same afternoon in the same place, Harold was crowned.

The coronation of kings and queens of England has evolved, but the ceremony then was the same in essence as it is today, a mixture of Germanic pomp and Christian blessing which was already ancient tradition. Now, it seems a theatrical performance of archaic rites, but then every part of it had a meaning and purpose everyone understood. It defined the duties of people, church and king, and set the king apart from all other men in a human office that was uniquely holy. The archbishop or a bishop asked the people if they accepted the king, and they acclaimed him with shouts of 'Vivat!' The king took a triple oath, of peace to his people, justice and mercy. The archbishop anointed his head and shoulders and hands with oil, amid prayers that further defined the duties of kingship – to defend the church and people and defy the infidel. Then came the investiture with the regalia, symbols of secular power, the ring of unity, the sword of protection, the crown of glory and justice, the sceptre of virtue and the rod of equity; and finally the benediction. Choirs sang the anthems they sing today, 'Let thy hand be strengthened', 'Zadok the Priest', 'Te Deum Laudamus', 'Vivat Rex in Eternum'.

Harold's coronation may have been hastily arranged, and perhaps subdued by the funeral in the morning and the grave still scarcely covered in the pavement before the altar. None the less, he emerged from it bound to the church and people by mutual oaths that the English had revered for many centuries past.

Long afterwards, his opponents hinted that the haste of it was indecent, as if he had been afraid someone else would snatch the crown from him. But there was a good traditional reason for doing it then and there. Coronations were held at the great feasts of the church, and the funeral was on Epiphany; if it had not been done that same afternoon, the bishops would have wanted to wait until Easter, leaving the kingdom without a head for what might be a difficult three months.

But it was certainly a strange situation that England had a new anointed king before anyone outside London knew the old king was dead, and within a week or so there was news that people in the north were complaining they had not been properly consulted. Perhaps the witan had gone a little too far. Without the mechanism of democracy which was far in the future, the witan were as truly the spokesmen of England as anyone could be; they were bound by oaths of justice perhaps more compelling than any oath could be today, and if they fell too far short in their people's eyes they were subject to the fate of Tostig. But the gemot had one inevitable weakness: when travel was slow and difficult, districts near the meeting place were bound to be better represented than districts far away. Since the witan met wherever the king was and Edward had never been to the north, no national gemot within memory had been held in the northern earldoms of Mercia or Northumbria. The two teenage earls, the brothers Edwin and Morkere, had been present in Thorney Island, and the Archbishop of York, which was the capital of Northumbria, had anointed the king; yet when they went home, their people seem to have said they would not accept the decision unless they were formally asked.

Harold's response was what one would expect: he rode at once to York, where Edward had never ventured. It was no warlike expedition, not even a display of strength. No doubt he took an escort, but he did not take an army: he took his friend Wulfstan, the saintly Bishop of Worcester. So he offered himself to the mercy of the northerners. A gemot of the earldoms was summoned in York and Wulfstan spoke to it. It was happily convinced, acclaimed Harold king and swore its oaths of fealty. So every part of England had had its say. Without any question, Harold was England's choice; and when it came to the test a few months later, the English fought for him without a single traitor.

There is a story that on this visit to York he made a choice of his own: a wife. The lady was Ealdgyth, who was sister of the two young earls, and she had led a melodramatic life.

Their father Aelfgar had been a permanently troublesome earl, one of the men whom Edward exiled, then forgave, then exiled again. On his second exile, in 1058, he went to Ireland, and then tried to return by making an alliance with Gruffydd (or Griffith), the King of Wales, who was fighting a perennial border war against Edward. To mark the alliance he gave his daughter Ealdgyth to the Welsh King as wife. Four years later, in 1062, he died, and in spite of his disgraceful behaviour Edward appointed his elder son to the earldom of Mercia. A year after that, in 1063, Harold invaded Wales on Edward's behalf and defeated Gruffydd's army. Gruffydd was killed, not by Harold but by his own people, and his widow was brought back to England.

The story that Harold married her is mentioned very briefly by a few of the historians, mainly Normans, as if they had heard of it only as a rumour. None of them says when or where it happened. Some seem to assume it was soon after Gruffydd's death, and if so one might imagine it as a romantic affair, with Harold rescuing the young princess from her bondage. But one cannot believe that Harold was allied to the northern earls by marriage before he was crowned, and that neither the *Vita* nor the Anglo-Saxon Chronicle mentioned it. Nor does Ealdgyth appear as queen in accounts of the coronation, or in any of the records of his reign, or in Domesday Book as the holder of any land in his earldom. It is slightly more plausible that he married her after he was crowned, on his visit to York. Alliance then with the earls was an urgent political need, and a marriage that united the north and south of England was the best foundation for a dynasty. But the wedding of a king was unlikely to pass without notice.

There was also Edith Svanneshals, who had been his lover for years, or perhaps rather more than his lover. There was a tacit arrangement for men of power to marry for love in their youth and marry again for politics when they were older. The first was called a Danish marriage; it was not blessed by the church and so was not irrevocable. The monks who wrote histories tended to disapprove of 'Danish' wives and call them concubines, and so did the historians of the nineteenth century, but socially and legally they had a respectable status. Knut's first marriage must have been this kind, and the son of it, the other Harold, was thought a legitimate heir to the kingdom. Edith was probably also a 'Danish' wife, but she was no legal bar to a marriage of convenience.

Personally, on the meagre evidence there is, I think it is unlikely that Harold really married Ealdgyth. If he had, there would have been a more positive comment on it somewhere. On the other hand, it is likely enough he discussed it on the visit to York, and even intended to do it. Ealdgyth has crept into the history books as queen of England, while Edith Svanneshals is dismissed as Harold's mistress. Yet it was Edith who performed the last act of love when he died, and her sons who led later armies to try to avenge their father.

Whatever he intended, time ran out. 'In that year,' the Anglo-Saxon Chronicle says, 'Harold was hallowed King; and he enjoyed little quiet while he ruled the realm.' Within ten days of the coronation, a threatening message came from Duke William of Normandy.

Rouen

January 10

The news had reached Normandy very quickly: it was taken across the Channel by a messenger in an English ship. Duke William was in a park near his capital city of Rouen when the messenger found him, with a crowd of the men of his court preparing for a hunt: he had strung his bow and handed it to a page to carry. (The story is in the *Roman de Rou*, a Norman history in verse that was written a hundred years later, and it may have some poetic licence.) The coronation had followed so soon on the death of the King that the messenger brought the news of both together: 'King Edward is dead, and Harold is raised to the kingdom.' The Duke abandoned the hunting: he looked angry, laced and unlaced his cloak: he spoke to nobody, and nobody dared to speak to him. He crossed the river Seine in a boat and went into the hall of his palace, and sat down on a bench with his head against a pillar and the cloak across his face. After a while his seneschal or steward came in, humming a tune, a man called William FitzOsbern who was a trusted friend. People asked him what had happened to upset the Duke. The Duke heard his voice and looked up, and FitzOsbern said it was no good trying to hide the news, people knew it already all over the city. There was no time for grieving, something had to be done.

Just as one had to look back at English history to appreciate the witan's dilemma in London, so one must now look briefly back at Norman history to explain the shock of the news in Rouen.

Normandy was a small country, no bigger than one of the English earldoms. It extended from Mont St Michel in the west to Le Tréport on the river Bresnes in the east, a distance of a hundred and sixty miles, and inland about half-way up the Seine between the sea and Paris. Its people, like the English, were partly of Viking stock; but England had been invaded mainly by Danish Vikings, and Normandy – with parts of Scotland and Ireland – by Norwegian Vikings who came on their raids round the north of Scotland and down the Irish Sea. It was surrounded by other countries without the Norman blood – Brittany, Maine, Anjou, Flanders, Ponthieu, Burgundy, Aquitaine – all under fiercely independent dukes and counts whose alliances and enmities were for ever changing, and whose allegiance to the King of France was as often broken as observed.

No doubt the peasants of Normandy were very much the same sort of people as the peasants of England, and its villages the same sort of places as Horstede. Its social system too was fundamentally the same as England's, in that everyone held his plot of land in duty to someone higher; everyone was bound by allegiance to a lord, and expected the lord's protection. But it was entirely different in spirit, in the way the system worked. The Norman aristocracy and their neighbours were much more warlike people. It was partly through necessity: with long land borders, no lord could survive unless he was able and willing to fight off other predatory lords. But it was also a matter of temperament: they loved fighting, while the English – or at least a significant number of them – had begun to discover the pleasure of having nobody to fight. England was unfortified, except for the walls or palisades round towns and important houses, which were designed to keep out robbers and animals rather than armies; but in Normandy every landlord or baron had his castle, designed to withstand a siege. And there was another important difference: the English had conceived the idea that every man, even the king, was subject to the law, but the Normans had not. The English were feeling their way, however dimly, towards a kind of democracy; the Normans towards efficient autocracy.

There was an added reason for the warlike nature of the Norman lords: they were imbued with chivalry, which had swept across northern Europe from an obscure beginning somewhere in Germany, but had not crossed the sea to England. In the following century, at the time of the crusades, chivalry became an international brotherhood with peculiar religious rites and esoteric morality. But at this time, as its name implies, it was nothing more than a cult of horsemanship and war.

On the mainland of northern Europe in that era, an aristocratic boy had to choose his life's ambition when he was seven or eight. The choice was to be a churchman or a chevalier, which later in England came to be called a knight. Book learning was left to the churchmen; those who chose to be knights began right away on a training that lasted until they were men. First they were pages, who waited on their master at table and at the hunt, and on their mistress in her bower; they were taught the fear of God by the chaplain, the arts of love by the ladies of the court, the arts of hunting by the master's huntsmen and of fighting by his knights. At sixteen they became squires, and learned to ride in armour and handle a lance and sword, and then to attend a knight in whatever battles were going. Finally in their early twenties they were admitted to the pride and dignity of knighthood.

Chivalry in later ages may have had merits, but in the eleventh century it was a social disaster. It produced a superfluity of conceited illiterate young men who had no ideals except to ride and hunt and fight, whose only interest in life was violence and the glory they saw in it. They were no good at anything else, and despised any peaceful occupation. In national wars they could be called on to fight by their feudal obligations, much like the thanes in England. But just by existing, they created wars. When they had nothing to do, they became mercenary soldiers who for pay and plunder, and for their own amusement, would form an army for anyone who wanted to start a private war. What was worse, perhaps, they were taught to look down on anyone who was not a knight, and they treated mere peasants or tradesmen with cruelty and disdain. Knighthood put an impassable barrier across the middle of the ranks of society.

The English had refused to fight each other in civil war, even when Edward ordered them to do it; but the unlucky Normans, at almost the same time, were ravaged again and again by wars of every size, from national invasions down to the private quarrels of neighbouring barons who hired bodies of knights to attack each other. They were wars which were usually inconclusive, because the defence was always stronger than the attack: it was not at all difficult to build an impregnable castle. Attackers tried first to take a castle or a walled town by surprise, and get inside before the gates were shut or the drawbridges raised. If they failed in that, there was nothing much more they could do except starve it out, or try to bribe the defenders or frighten them into submission by burning surrounding buildings and destroying crops. While the sieges went on, the countryside between the castles was more or less undefended, and knights could ride around it fighting occasional skirmishes, plotting ambushes and ingenious deceits and doing whatever damage they liked to anyone and anything they found there.

The knights themselves delighted in these affairs: the people who suffered were the peasants who happened to get in the way. For their sake, the church did its best to control the incessant violence. Knowing in its wisdom that men would always fight, it decreed the remarkable concept known as the Truce of God, by which wars were forbidden in Lent and on certain saints' days and also, every week, from Wednesday evening to Monday morning. The Truce of God existed and was more or less effective in various parts of Europe all through the eleventh and twelfth centuries, and it was imposed in Normandy in 1042. Thereafter, peasants could warily till their fields three days in the week and rest undisturbed on Sundays, but they were wise to take cover on Mondays, Tuesdays and Wednesdays, when knights might come thundering through the crops intent on their quest for glory.

William was born in this turbulent world in 1027 or 1028. His father, the previous Duke of Normandy, was known as Robert the Devil, and William himself in his lifetime as William the Bastard; for Robert had caught the eye of a girl named Herleve or Arlette who was the daughter of a tanner in the town of Falaise. (William seems not to have minded the title – bastardy ran in the family – but he was extremely angry in later life when enemies pretended he stank of the tannery.) Not long after William was born, Robert decided to make the pilgrimage to the Holy Land, and before he went on the dangerous journey it was necessary to decide the succession to the Dukedom. The procedure was not the same as England's. He called a meeting of the powerful men and presented William as his heir, saying with perhaps a hint of apology that he was small but would grow. The assembly did not like the choice but it could not agree on any other; it reluctantly paid homage to the child. Robert then set off on his journey and died on the way, and at the age of seven William became the Duke of Normandy.

The country fell to pieces at once. Central authority was defied and disappeared. Every minor baron set himself up as an independent sovereign, extorted taxes, collected what knights he could and declared his own wars. There was frantic activity in building stronger castles. Anarchy, devastation and slaughter were worse than they had ever been before. The fine distinction between war and murder disappeared, and enemies were done to death with poison, trickery and daggers in the night. The poor became destitute. The guardians Robert had appointed for his son were poisoned or stabbed by one faction or another or thrown into dungeons, and for years, to save his own life, he was hidden and moved from place to place by his mother's family.

Not many people can ever have had a more precarious childhood, so bereft of the safety and continuity children need. He began to grow up with precocious signs of a genius for the politics of violence.

Perhaps the Truce of God, when he was fourteen, gave him a little more freedom to be boyish, but when he was sixteen he was thought fit to be knighted, and when he was eighteen the barons sensed a danger that he would soon be stronger and tougher than any of them. So they combined, and staged a full-sized revolution.

It divided the country in two. The western part, which was predominantly Norse, was in revolt; the eastern part, more French, was loyal to William. When it broke out, William happened to be in the rebel part, but he was woken in the night and warned to fly for his life. He rode a night and a day across country and reached the house of a friend; and in the *Roman de Rou* there is an early example of a perennial story. Pursuers came pounding up and asked which way the Bastard had gone. 'He went thataway,' the loyal friend replied, pointing in the wrong direction; and was rewarded, years later, by having his son appointed Sheriff of Essex.

William himself was vassal or liege of the King of France, and in this crisis he asked for his protection. The King came into Normandy with a French army, and in 1047 he and William met the rebels near the city of Caen. The battle was memorable because – although there were foot soldiers present – it was fought entirely by mounted knights who charged each other with lances, shields and swords. With the help of the King, William won: at nineteen, all the barons of Normandy swore allegiance to him, paid fines, gave hostages and agreed to demolish illicit castles, and all except one were forgiven for their crimes.

For the next decade, William fought to preserve the power he had won, and slowly changed anarchy to prosperity. It was not that fighting ever stopped, far from it; but he put an end to the private wars which had done most damage in the country, and as opposition dwindled in Normandy he began to wage his own wars outside his frontiers, letting the knights work off their energy in fields where other peasants, not Normans, were the ones to suffer. He invaded and conquered Maine, fought sometimes for the King of France and sometimes against him, and won a grudging allegiance from the neighbouring counts of Brittany and Ponthieu. Norman knights enrolled in victorious armies as far away as Sicily and Spain, while Normandy was often left in peace like the calm in the eye of a hurricane.

It was a peace enforced by William's own decrees, not by a formal system of law and justice. Normandy had no written law, as England had had for many generations. But he won a reputation for just decisions; he set himself aims that were usually wise, and carried them out, if he had to, by means that were ruthless. He cowed the barons by his own more powerful personality, and controlled the knights by being as good a fighter as any.

He also controlled the church. It was ironic but true that the church in Normandy was strengthened by the excesses of the knights. From choice they played with sudden death, but everyone in that era lived in fear of God, and they did not risk damnation. Before their fights they devoutly prayed for success, and if it was granted they gave thanks to the church, and donations from their booty; and when they grew too old to fight, it seems that many were remorseful, endowed new churches and even took the vows of monks. William himself could not rule without the support of the church; so he defended it strongly and earned its blessing. He presided at its synods, approved or disapproved its laws and appointed its bishops. Some of his choices were foreigners who were renowned for their learning, but some were members of his family who would do as they were told – most notable among them his half-brother Odo, who was as warlike as any Norman but was created Bishop of Bayeux, improbable though it seems, when he could not have been much older than thirteen.

In 1066, when William was thirty-eight or thirty-nine, he had spent the whole of his life since childhood – probably every day of it – either in war or the sports that were training for war, or the warlike rule that was the prize of victory. He was probably illiterate, devoid of any intellectual or artistic interest, God-fearing, just when he was not angry, and absolutely intolerant. He was a more barbarous primitive man than either Edward or Harold, but he is not to be blamed: he came from a more barbarous primitive country. Autocracy is always an over-simplification of the art of government; but that was what Normandy needed, and humble men following teams of oxen up the Norman furrows had reason to be grateful.

It was not what England needed. The Anglo-Saxon Chronicle has an eloquent obituary, which was written in the year he died. 'If anyone wants to know what kind of man he was, we will write of him as we understood him who knew him and at one time lived at his court. He was very clever and very powerful, stronger and more dignified than any of his predecessors. He was mild to good men who loved God, and beyond all measure severe to men who opposed his will. He was rigid and cruel, put earls in bondage who had acted against his wishes, cast bishops from their bishoprics and abbots from their abbacies, and thanes into prison . . . caused castles to be built and poor men to be terribly oppressed . . . He cared nothing for the hatred of them all. Alas that any man should be so proud, so raise himself up and account himself above all other men! May Almighty God show mercy to his soul and grant him forgiveness of his sins!' Yet even the Chronicle of the people he conquered added the saving virtue: 'Among everything else, we must remember the peace he kept in the land.'

Before that January day in 1066, Duke William had never had to think of conquering England. On the contrary, he had believed for many years that Edward had promised him the crown, and that when Edward died the English would happily welcome him as king. It seems a sincere belief, and it was probably true, or at least half true: Edward, in his vague and unpractical way, had said something to William that could be taken as a promise. Some Norman histories say the promise was made before Edward left Normandy, but it is hard to believe Edward promised the crown to William before he possessed it himself, and when William was only a boy. A likelier time was in 1051, when William visited England while Godwin and his family were in exile. The Norman histories are full of the promise but do not mention the visit, while one English chronicle describes the visit but none of them mention the promise; but this was the only occasion when Edward and William met while Edward was King and when William was grown-up.

The whole thing was a misunderstanding, either by William or by both: whatever either of them thought at the time, no king of England had a right to promise the crown. The kingdom was not a private estate (as Normandy may have been) to be handed on by an owner's will to a chosen heir: it was the people of England, represented by the witan, who had the final constitutional right to choose a king. Yet this misunderstanding was the root cause of the Norman conquest, and it is only too easy to see how it may have happened.

William came to England on that visit in 1051 with a large, imposing retinue, a handsome young man (he was twenty-three) who was already making order out of the chaos in Normandy and proving himself a prodigy as a ruler – exactly the kind of person to waken Edward's impulsive affection. He arrived at the crucial moment when Edward had got rid of Godwin and his family – he hoped for ever – and was entirely surrounded by his Norman favourites. William's reception at court was a purely Norman feast: to him, to Edward, to the Norman bishops Edward had appointed, and to the courtiers with their new-won power, England seemed at that brief moment to be destined to be ruled by Normans. In the euphoria of the party it was natural to think of England and Normandy united happily in the future under William's efficient rule. Perhaps they thought the witan would welcome such a splendid plan; more likely they thought the English constitution and English opinion no longer mattered much. Possibly Edward did not mean to make a binding promise. Possibly he remembered the limit of his right and only promised to recommend William to the witan when the time came. But whatever he said, he let William go home believing the kingdom would be his when Edward died.

This also seems the only moment when Wulfnoth, Godwin's youngest son, could have fallen into William's power, as he certainly did. It was the custom to confirm agreements by exchanging hostages. Edward demanded hostages of Godwin when they quarrelled, and since Godwin lost the quarrel his hostages would have been forfeit. Wulfnoth was not mentioned as having gone into exile with his father and brothers, and he disappeared from history until he was released when William died. The only conceivable cause of his fate is that Godwin offered him as hostage to Edward and perforce had to leave him behind when he fled the country – and that Edward, to seal a bargain of his own, handed him over to William, who took him away to Normandy. The same thing happened to another of Godwin's family: Hakon, who is thought to have been Godwin's grandson, the bastard son of Svein. The presence of these unlucky boys in Normandy, under restraint if not in prison, is a strong indication that some agreement was made between Edward and William.

All this happened fifteen years before 1066, and England, soon after the bargain was made, changed firmly back to being English. Godwin returned, the Norman favourites were routed, and Edward himself in the next few years became more English in outlook and gave a trust and affection to Godwin's sons and daughter that he had never given to Godwin himself. It grew ever more certain, as time went on, that the witan would never willingly accept a foreign king. Yet Edward seems never to have confessed to anyone English exactly what he had said to William, or to have told William that things had changed since they met. That was his way. It was like him to make a vague promise, wrapped up in a mass of pious circumlocution, and then to persuade himself he had never made it, or to hope it would be forgotten. It was probably not the only time he had done it. King Swein of Denmark also said in 1066 that Edward had promised him the crown; but he was a cousin and friend of Harold, and he did not press the claim.

During those fifteen years, William must have begun to suspect that Edward's promise was not worth very much, and that the English had a will of their own and a constitutional way of expressing it. But in 1064, something else happened which renewed his belief.

This is a much more debatable story, the story that Harold went to Normandy to confirm the promise and swore a solemn oath to William that he would support him as king – the story held by the Normans in 1066 to be proof that Harold was a perjurer and usurper whom William was morally bound to attack and kill. It is not told at all in English chronicles, but every historian after the conquest told it – at least five Normans, including the designer of the Bayeux tapestry, and four of the rather later Anglo-Norman writers in England. Evidently, it seemed to the Normans a very important affair, and one may infer that William's attack on England was widely criticized and the consciences of Normans were uneasy. It is important still if one wants to understand the psychological causes of the conquest.

But all the versions of the tale are different and contradictory. Modern historians for a century past have analysed the versions word by word to try to deduce what really happened, but have never quite succeeded: it is an entertaining puzzle, and still insoluble. All one can do is tell the essence of the Norman account, add its variations, subtract what is plainly impossible, and make the best judgement one can of what remains.

The most extreme form of the story is the earliest, which was written down between 1072 and 1074 by the Duke's chaplain, William of Poitiers. He begins by saying that Harold was sent to Normandy by Edward, specifically to confirm that William should be king. He sailed from his home, which was at Bosham on Chichester harbour, and was driven ashore by a storm, not in Normandy but on the neighbouring coast of the Count of Ponthieu, who was one of William's vassals. The count put Harold in prison, but William heard of it and demanded his release. Harold was then made welcome at William's palace at Rouen, and he accompanied William on a warlike foray against his neighbours in Brittany. William knighted him in the Norman fashion, and Harold took an oath that he would be William's liege or 'his man', would represent him at Edward's court and would use all his influence and resources to secure the crown for him when Edward died. In the meantime, he would hand over the town of Dover to William's soldiers, fortify it and supply the garrison's needs at his own expense; likewise with other towns that William might wish to have fortified in other parts of the kingdom. William, in return, confirmed Harold in his honours and earldom. Finally Harold was allowed to go home, laden with gifts and taking with him one but only one of the hostages William held : his nephew Hakon, but not his brother Wulfnoth.

The only parts of this version which run through all the others are the departure from Bosham, the storm that drove Harold ashore, the expedition to Brittany, and the fact that Harold swore an oath of some sort. In later accounts, the motive for the journey is completely changed. One says it was not that Edward sent Harold on a royal mission, but that Harold himself decided to go to Normandy in the hope of persuading William to release the hostages, and Edward warned him he would only get himself into trouble. Other chroniclers said both these reasons were wrong: Harold did not intend to cross the Channel at all, he was only going on a fishing and hunting trip, and was blown out to sea and wrecked on the other side.

The story of the oath is also changed. Some say it was sworn at Rouen, some at Bayeux and some at Bonneville; some after the expedition to Brittany and some before it. The political promises fade out of the story until one is left in the end with nothing more than a promise that Harold would marry one of William's daughters, or that he would give his own sister to marry a Norman noble. But something is also added: the story that the oath was sworn at a table, and that William secretly hid the relics of Norman saints underneath it (or in a chest) to trick Harold into binding himself more strongly. This is a Norman addition, told to show William's cleverness, not an English one to show his deceitfulness. The Bayeux tapestry shows the scene of the oath, with the holy relics, but says nothing about the promises.

Putting all the versions together, one has to conclude that Harold did go to Normandy, after being cast ashore on the short strip of coast, near the town of St Valery, which belonged to the Count of Ponthieu: this much is as certain as any of the history of the era. The only time he could have done it was in the summer of 1064.

Of the reasons for the journey, the least likely is that Edward sent him: if the King had sent the premier earl of the country on such a foreign mission, the fact must have been well known in England and either recorded at the time or remembered in later annals. Nor is there any mention in any account of the aristocratic entourage an earl would have taken on such a royal mission. It is possible he went with the King's permission to try to release his brother, and failed; but on every count it is most likely the journey was an accident.

This part of the problem needs a sailor's eye. The Bayeux tapestry shows him embarking at Bosham, and he is taking with him hawks and hounds. It also says he was driven ashore on the coast of the Count of Ponthieu 'with the wind full in his sails', which implies he was caught in a gale from west or north. The crossing from Bosham to the Norman coast is under a hundred miles, and William's domain was a hundred and sixty miles long (see endpaper map). If Harold had wanted to go to Normandy, it is hard to conceive that in any change of wind – even in the ships of that era, which could only sail with the wind abaft the beam – he could neither have reached the Norman coast nor put back to some place on the coast of England.

But if he did not want to go to Normandy, the thing makes nautical sense. If he was fishing off the Isle of Wight, or going hunting in the forests to the west, and was caught off his own harbour by a northerly gale, he would have tried to claw his way back to the English coast, heading as best he could for the Straits of Dover. In those conditions he might very well have been driven farther off shore and finished up at St Valery. This is not conclusive, nothing is; but at least it makes a story a sailor can believe. The imprisonment after the shipwreck is also believable: any casual mariner cast ashore on a foreign coast in those days, and long afterwards, was liable to be treated as a pirate and held to ransom, and the richer the captive the better; but it would not have happened to an earl with his retinue travelling on the business of a king.

All the versions in their different ways suggest that Harold and William took an instant liking to each other. They had never met before, they were almost the same age (Harold a year or two the older), both of high rank and reputation. In character, they were a contrast: each, so to speak, was the end-product of the country he was born in – Harold the patient conciliator, William the man of decision. William made an excellent host: Harold distinguished himself in the fighting in Brittany, was charmed by William's wife the Duchess Matilda and her family, and had some reason to be grateful to William for getting him out of the dungeons of Ponthieu.

Yet behind the show of friendship there is a suspicion that Harold was as much a prisoner as a guest. He had lost his ships and presumably, after being wrecked and imprisoned, he had to borrow everything, clothes, horses, weapons and even money. He could not go home unless William helped him. The Count of Ponthieu had imprisoned him and William had imprisoned his brother: there was no reason why William should not imprison him too and use him to extract some vast kind of ransom from England – perhaps the abdication of Edward. This might be no more than a suspicion if it were not for two incidents: William's trickery with the saints' relics, and his refusal to liberate Harold's brother. Both indicate that William was making the best of a chance that put Harold in his power.

So one comes to the oath, the central part of the story. One of the promises alleged against Harold by William of Poitiers is so outrageously improbable that one can simply refuse to believe it. Harold could not have promised 'in the meantime' – that is, while Edward was still alive – to fortify Dover and other towns for garrisons of Norman soldiers. If he had done it alone, it would have been treason and instantly lost him his earldom and his power. If Edward had approved and they had seriously tried to do it together, it would certainly have started a revolution. Nor could William have been so naïve as to ask for this promise or believe it. It can only be a tale misunderstood and magnified by Norman propagandists to discredit Harold.

This exaggeration throws doubt on all the rest, and perhaps the other important promise, that Harold would use his influence to secure the crown for William when Edward died, was equally malicious and untrue. But nobody ever denied he promised something, and this at least was in his power to promise. There are two opposite reasons why he might have done it, and anyone may make a choice between them.

The first is that Harold made this promise with no intention of keeping it because it was the only way he could escape from

Normandy. If he did, he gave William a powerful excuse for the attack on England two years later, but that was a result he could not have foreseen at the time.

The other, which with some hesitation I favour on the whole, is that a real friendship had sprung up between them: a calculating friendship perhaps, but none the less sincere. This presupposes that Harold had seen no prospect then, in 1064, that the witan might choose him king. He expected to spend his life as second-in-command, just as his father had spent his, first ruling the country on behalf of cantankerous Edward and then, most probably, on behalf of Edgar, an unpredictable boy. What William offered was really more attractive. William, a man of his own age and experience, a proven genius as a ruler, would make a delightful change from Edward and a more understanding colleague than Edgar. England and Normandy in friendly union would be a very powerful state. William would be the nominal ruler, and Harold the *de facto* ruler of England, with more independence than he could have had under a native king. It may have seemed to him, in the exuberance of a sudden friendship, a glittering prospect not only for himself but for England too. One cannot say he would have been wrong, if the English had been willing to accept the idea. But they were not.

It is quite possible that Harold did fulfil this promise. In the lobbying among the witan when Edward was dying, it is not recorded who was in favour of whom. Harold may have done his best and spoken up for William, either then or at any time in the past two years, and found that a majority of the witan would not consider William or any foreign king at any price. That was all he was said to have promised to do, and all he could do: the decision belonged to the witan. William, the absolute autocrat, may well have believed that if Edward the king and Harold the premier earl both wanted him to succeed, the thing was as good as settled – but that was not how England worked. It was a wrongful extension of the promise to say, as the Normans said afterwards, that Harold should have refused to reign when the witan chose him to do it; for he certainly knew by then that if he refused, the witan's second choice would be Edgar, not William. The glittering plan turned out to be impossible.

With nine different versions of this complicated story, one can go on for ever trying to follow up the possible trains of thought of William and Harold. For what it is worth, my own conclusion is this: Harold arrived in Normandy by accident in 1064, he and William came to like and admire each other, Harold saw an advantage for himself and England in peacefully uniting the two domains with William as king of both and himself as Subregulus in England, and he promised to do his best to bring it about. Possibly he did do his best but could not persuade the witan; and it would have been better for England if he had succeeded.

All that is a matter of opinion. There is only one certain thing: whatever he promised, he could not have meant to put himself under an obligation to oppose the witan's constitutional decision when they made it, whatever it was. No Englishman could have done that. But still, an oath sworn on the relics of saints was a very solemn affair, even if it was sworn under duress or through a misunderstanding, and even if it proved impossible to carry out; and Harold's conscience, I think, was uneasy about it for the rest of his life.

Returning now to that winter's day in Rouen, one can feel the shock that reduced the Duke to silence and understand the psychological problem it presented. For fifteen years, he had believed he was heir to England. The belief had begun to wear thin, but then it had been renewed by Harold's visit. The news that Edward was dead was not unexpected: the shock was that Harold had been crowned at once, and William had not been warned or consulted or given any chance to make his claim. It might not have mattered so much if it had been a purely personal disappointment, but it was far more than that. All those years, he had let it be known in Normandy and in the courts of Europe that he was Edward's heir. Every Norman from his barons to his ploughmen knew their Duke expected to be King of England. He could not accept the news and do nothing without losing face, without being made to look foolish. Was it too late?

Could the news be kept secret, at least till he tried to prove his case in England? No: FitzOsbern the seneschal came in and told him everyone in Rouen knew what had happened, already they were waiting to see what he would do. His power rested on his reputation of strength: the one thing he could not possibly afford was to be laughed at. He was trapped from that moment by his own pride and eminence, forced into an act of defiance, a dangerous enterprise he could never have wanted – and ultimately into a long career of cruel oppression which made him ashamed in his later life whenever he paused to think of it.

The Comet

April 18

William sent the message to Harold at once. One cannot discover much of what it said, whether it was written or oral, angry or dismayed: he begged, asked or demanded that Harold should fulfil his promises – and each historian made the message fit his own version of the promises. It seems he could hardly believe what had happened, and wanted to hear about it from Harold himself, still hoping perhaps that it was nothing irrevocable. But Harold's reply was adamant: the witan had chosen him king and the church had anointed him. It may have been then that Harold first offered the excuse which appeared in later chronicles: that if he had sinned, the sin was in making the promises, not in his failure to keep them, since they had proved impossible to keep.

Then, according to some of the accounts, William sent a second message: would Harold at least fulfil the promise to marry his daughter? This is one of the strangest of Norman reports, suggesting as it does that William was still willing to be friendly.

The whole business of the promised marriage is intriguing. It was clearly not another bastard that William was said to have offered, but a daughter of his wife Matilda. (Unlike so many of these people, William had no recorded bastard children, nor any previous 'Danish' marriage.) He and Matilda had four sons and at least five daughters; but when Harold was in Normandy they had certainly not been married more than thirteen years and probably only eleven, after waiting four years for approval from the Pope. So the oldest of the children could only have been twelve, and was probably only ten – unless they had some before they were married, and that is unlikely, since it was a formal political marriage and Matilda was the daughter of the respected Count of Flanders. Furthermore, Harold's choice by all accounts was not the oldest, but the second or third, whose name was Agatha.

Diplomatic betrothals were often made between children, and often broken off before the children were old enough to marry. They were rarer between a girl of say eight or nine and a man over forty, but perhaps not quite impossible. Yet could Harold, whose own children by the faithful Edith were much older than Agatha, have been so uncivilized as to mean it seriously? It seems more the kind of thing a contented middle-aged guest might say to a pretty flirtatious little girl, perhaps as a sly compliment to her mother. One of the later versions has it that William used to go to bed early, leaving Harold and Matilda to sit up talking together; and when at last he grew rather angry and asked what they found to talk about, they told him they had thought of this betrothal. That at least is a scene one can imagine, for Harold had the reputation of a susceptible man and Matilda of an attractive woman with a strong personality – although when her tomb was opened in 1967 it was revealed that she herself was no bigger than an average eight-year-old, not more than fifty inches tall, or 1.39 metres.

At any rate, Harold could not decently have married the child until she came to puberty; so it could only have been a promise for the future, not one he could be accused in 1066 of having broken. Nor were these betrothals, or the breaking of them, usually considered very serious. What then could William's second message have been but his final expression of friendship, and Matilda's too – an offer even now to accept what Harold had done, to agree that he could not help it, to forget William's claim to the throne – if only he could tell his people he was allied with England and could expect his grandson to be king? What if Harold had answered yes, he still thought Agatha a charming little girl and would be happy to marry her when she grew up? Would the Norman conquest have been averted? Or had he committed himself in the meantime to Ealdgyth, the sister of his northern earls? If he had, he did not say so; he only replied that a King of England could not marry a foreigner without the witan's permission. It was not a conclusive answer, but it is intelligible: after all, he had made the promise as earl, and an earl could marry anyone he chose; while a king's marriage was bound to imply a political alliance. But in the other parallel Norman story, that he had offered his own sister in marriage to a Norman, his reply is made offensive and quite uncharacteristic: his sister was dead, and did Duke William want to be sent the corpse?

It is a muddle, like all the Norman stories about Harold, and the more one looks at it the worse the muddle becomes. In the end, one cannot do more than make another intuitive guess. The most plausible guess, I believe, is that the betrothal had indeed been discussed as a friendly light-hearted pleasantry; that William, when he finally became exasperated with Harold, added it as a makeweight to his complaints against him; and that his propagandists, seeking to justify the projected invasion, blew it up into a nightmarish travesty of itself. For after William's second message, he and his spokesmen set to work methodically, cleverly and thoroughly to blacken Harold's character, and the broken betrothal became a case of blasphemous perjury.

Yet Ordericus Vitalis, who wrote his history seventy years afterwards, added a final episode, and another dimension, to the story. In 1074, when she might have been seventeen, poor Agatha was offered again in marriage, this time to a King Alfonso of Castile who was her father's ally of the moment; and on the way to Spain for her wedding she died. It was the mercy of God, Ordericus said, that she was released from a fate she hated; for she still remembered Harold as the only man she had ever wanted to marry.

It does look as if Harold, in this exchange of messages, missed a chance of conciliation, much the most important in his life; he fell short of his reputation for soothing people's feelings. But perhaps no king should be expected to start his reign with an apology. As a man, Harold might frankly have said he was very sorry, but the plans he had made with William had turned out to be impossible; he might have thought of a face-saving compromise. But as king he was bound to consult his advisers, the leaders of the witan; and the witan had nothing to be apologetic about.

He certainly knew within a month of his coronation that he had made a mortal enemy and could not hope to be left to reign in peace, in spite of the PAX he ordered to be inscribed on his coinage. He began to try to rouse the people to a sense of danger, at least in the vulnerable part of southern England. The English have never liked to prepare for trouble before they can see it in front of their faces, and in 1066 they took a lot of persuading that anything had to be done. But by early summer, in the words of the Anglo-Saxon Chronicle, he had 'gathered such a great naval force, and a land force also, as no other king in the land had gathered before.'

A King of England had two kinds of men to make an army. First there were house-carls, who were professional regular soldiers. Kings and earls all had their own house-carls, and Harold had a double force because he remained the Earl of Wessex. These men were either ignorant or scornful of the techniques of chivalry, and they fought on foot in the way they had learned from the Vikings, with massive and bloodthirsty two-handed axes and swords. They had a fearsome reputation: even a saga from Norway, the home of Vikings, said in that century that one English house-carl was worth two other soldiers. But there were not many of them: professional armies were too expensive. Old chronicles seldom give figures, but it is doubtful that Harold could muster more than two thousand of his own, and a few hundred more from his brothers Gyrth and Leofwine, whose earldoms adjoined his own and extended from Kent to Norfolk.

A much larger part of the army was the fyrd, which was part-time and amateur – the citizen army in which Ulfer the thane of Horstede was obliged by his tenure of land to serve up to two months a year. Beside the thanes, each hundred was expected to produce a few volunteers for the fyrd, and it has been reckoned that around fifty thousand men in the country were liable to this service. But the call-up was more or less local, and nothing like all of them could ever have been assembled in one place. They were not so heavily armed as the house-carls – it must have needed exceptional muscles and practice to fight with a two-handed axe – and they had the virtues and faults of any part-time army. Among their faults in 1066 was presumably a lack of practical experience. The house-carls had recently fought under Harold's leadership in Wales; but the fyrd of southern England had not seen a battle for half a century.

Even more locally, any and every able-bodied man would turn out to fight if his own home was threatened. All armies, when a battle seemed imminent, acquired a fringe of the neighbouring peasants, ready to do or die with hunting spears and knives and home-made clubs.

Raising a navy was a different problem. All the kings of England after Alfred had a few ships of their own, but not nearly enough for war: when they needed a warlike fleet, they chartered whatever merchant ships they could get, with their merchant crews, and put soldiers on board them. Harold was worse off than most. As earl, he owned some ships at his home on Chichester harbour. But he inherited nothing much as King. In 1050, Edward had possessed fourteen royal ships, but he paid them off and remitted the tax that had been levied to support them.

However, Edward, perhaps at Harold's suggestion, had made a better and more economical arrangement: he founded the Confederation of the Cinque Ports. The original Cinque Ports, all in Kent and Sussex, were Sandwich, Dover, Hythe, Romney and Hastings; others were added later in the Middle Ages. They were granted some rights of self-government, and undertook in return to provide a fleet for the King, without payment, for a certain number of days in the year: in later centuries, it was fifty-seven ships with their crews, free for fifteen days and at a fixed rate of charter for longer periods.

The unprecedented fleet that Harold gathered was therefore led by his own few ships, but the rest were the ordinary trading ships of the Cinque Ports, augmented from other harbours along the south coast. They were ships of Viking design, double-ended with the high curved stem and sternpost of Norse tradition; not the formidable longships that the Vikings built for war, but the broader and slower ships for carrying cargo. They came in all sizes up to sixty or seventy feet and carried a single square sail, but they could not sail to windward. In contrary winds, if their voyage was exceptionally urgent, they were rowed. Normally, in the patient manner of the medieval world, they just waited where they were for the wind to change or drifted with the tide.

By Easter, the call-up had spread a warning through southern England that trouble was brewing, but not through all of England. The fyrd was not summoned much farther inland than fifty miles, and in the midlands, well away from the coast, there were thousands of villages hidden away in woods and valleys where people had no reason to know that anything special was happening – people who lived through the whole of 1066 absorbed in their parochial affairs and undisturbed by anything more than distant rumours.

Horstede certainly knew about it, only twelve miles from the Channel coast. Ulfer the thane had gone, and probably taken a few of the sons of his tenants: so had the thane of Gorde and the other villages up and down the valley. They had gone to the tedious uneventful job of watching the coast – perhaps to Seaford, where Horstede's own river ran out to the sea, or to Pevensey on the other side of Beachy Head, which was a more important harbour, or possibly even as far as the Isle of Wight. Other men, making their way through the forest to the coast, came down the track along the valley carrying arms and stopped in Horstede to exchange their gossip, and beyond the river on the Roman road horsemen rode past more urgently than usual.

Yet one cannot imagine the people of Horstede were very much excited by it all; more likely they persuaded themselves, in the usual English way, that somebody high up was making a fuss about nothing and it would all turn out to be a false alarm. Easter was the biggest of all their annual feasts. That year it was on 16 April, and when they walked through the fields of spring to church that Sunday morning they had better and happier things to think about. Even now, in the second half of April, this part of England with all its blemishes is almost painfully beautiful. In the woods of Horstede the buds have subtly changed the outline of the oaks, the birches are already covered with a gauze of green, the cuckoo has come with its stupid summery song, the dismal English winter is past and everything is coming to life, the birds and animals and crops, and the men and women too: Christ is risen. It is not a time to take much heed of warnings.

But on the night of the Tuesday after Easter, something happened far worse than warnings of kings or threats of human enemies, something that amazed and overawed the Horstede people and shattered their springtime peace of mind. A monstrous light appeared in the sky, silently moving with a trail of fire. People went out to gaze at it in fear, then in again to examine their consciences and ask each other what it could portend. All over England it was seen that night and seven nights after. The King saw it, with what feelings one cannot know; so did the witan, assembled with him for the Easter feast on Thorney Island. Monks, more learned than most, said it was a star called cometa, the hairy star. Modern astronomers say it was Halley's comet. Whatever it was, everyone saw it as an omen of doom, a heavenly sign of wrath and fire on earth.

Sure enough, the comet had scarcely vanished when a strange fleet of ships was sighted off the Isle of Wight, and fierce foreign sailors came swarming ashore. But it was not the Duke of Normandy who led them, it was Harold's brother Tostig.

Of all the tragic figures of that year, Tostig is the most pathetic. What on earth did he hope to achieve? Since his earldom rebelled against him he had been six months in exile, living in Flanders where his wife was born, and where he had stayed with his father in that other exile fifteen years before. One may take it as certain that when his brother was crowned he hoped to be forgiven and welcomed home: it is equally certain that Harold could not have done anything of the kind – the loyalty of the northern earls was precarious enough, and to bring Tostig back would have been to ask for revolt. So Tostig's resentment may have been renewed. Yet to imagine he could land in England, right in the middle of Harold's earldom, with a small band of foreigners, and be welcomed there and build up a following which would challenge his brother – this was simply crazy.

All the evidence suggests that Tostig was really out of his mind. Sheer lunacy of course was recognized in those days, but the subtle gradations of mental sickness were not. Yet people must have suffered from them then as they do now, and history can be distorted if one always insists on finding sane and rational reasons for the things they did. Certainly if anyone behaved like Tostig now, he would be sent to a psychiatrist. His character had changed. He had been a charming young man whom everyone liked: Queen Edith's favourite brother, the hunting companion of the pious King, a man whom the critical author of the *Vita Aedwardi* could admire. Yet as earl, he had suddenly become secretive, impossibly cruel and domineering, even murderous. Accused of it, he had turned the accusation against his brother, without being able to offer evidence that made any impression on anyone at the time. He came to believe that everyone was involved in a plot against him, his own thanes, the humble people of his earldom, Harold, the court, the other earls, and finally Edward himself. And now he came back, in a forlorn and futile invasion that was quite out of touch with reality.

Before he landed in the Isle of Wight, he had sailed to Normandy. He may have counted on William's sympathy because his own wife Judith and William's wife Matilda were cousins, both of the family of the Counts of Flanders. He can only have been an embarrassment. William was busy with projects of his own, elaborate, vast and very carefully planned. Tostig's irrational plots were no possible help;

much less would William have confided his own precise intentions to an unbalanced man who seemed doomed to get himself killed or captured. So Tostig sailed again alone.

There is something specially pathetic in his choice of the Isle of Wight. It was where he had landed with his father on the return from that previous exile – where Harold had joined them from Ireland and the family was united again and they started their triumphant voyage along the coast to London, welcomed in every port they came to. Had he imagined a repetition of the triumph, the joyful celebrations and the heroic feasting? What he met was first bewilderment and then hostility. The people collected money and food for him, but it was not to make a feast, it was to pay him to go away, as people had paid the Vikings in the past.

He went, and began the same journey along the same coast, calling at the ports he remembered from that other time, Pevensey, Hastings, Romney, Dover and Sandwich. This may not have been his plan; he could not help it. He had crossed with a southerly wind and it stayed in the south: so when he reached the English coast he was pinned there and could not get off it again. The fyrd who were watching the ports were puzzled: they had been told to look out for Normans, not for the brother of the King. But everywhere, when they had time to consult each other, he was rejected and told to go somewhere else. When he needed provisions, he had to fight for them.

Harold was in London when this journey began, and his fleet was not ready yet. He marched through Kent with the house-carls, heading for Sandwich. Tostig heard he was coming and put to sea again, taking some local ships and their crews, some willingly and others by force. Again he was close to Flanders where he had left his wife and children and could at least find friendship. But the wind was still against him, and the only way he could go was north. He was heard of next in the Humber, where he went ashore to ravage and burn like the old invaders. Morkere and Edwin, the northern earls, turned out against him and fought him off, and most of his sailors deserted. At last he was left with only twelve small ships: the Chronicle calls them snaccum, which might mean fishing smacks. With that sad remnant, he disappeared again, still blown to the north, and asked for refuge from Malcolm, King of Scots.

When Tostig had gone and fear of the comet had begun to fade it was summer: peace descended again. Life went on as usual except on the south coast where the fyrd was gathered, and especially in the Isle of Wight; for there, where Tostig had made his first appearance, Harold assembled the whole of his navy and probably most of his army.

People have often assumed that Harold formed a navy in the hope of intercepting William's invading fleet at sea and fighting it there; but that is a misunderstanding of the nature of a medieval navy. There was no possible way of planning an interception at sea, and nobody ever attempted it before Sir Francis Drake, who proposed it as a revolutionary strategy when the Spanish Armada was coming.

All through the Middle Ages, when fleets could only sail with the wind on the beam or abaft it, the chance of two of them meeting at sea was so remote that sea fighting formed no part of the military art. Before 1066, there had been only one recorded battle at sea in English history: that was nearly two hundred years before, in 882, when an English fleet and a Danish fleet met by pure chance in the estuary of the Thames, neither suspecting that the other was there. The next sea battle – excepting the minor fights of pirates and one major battle in harbour – was nearly three centuries later, in 1350, and that also happened by chance. Mediterranean powers used fighting fleets of galleys rowed by slaves, but in northern Europe nobody deliberately planned to fight at sea until the beginning of naval artillery in the sixteenth century. The only exception was the Vikings. They sometimes fought in their ships – not against anyone else, because they had no rivals, but only against each other, among the fjords and islands of their homelands.

With that exception, medieval navies were not assembled for fighting other navies, their only purpose was transporting armies; and that is the only use of a navy that Harold could possibly have contemplated. It is a reasonable guess that he gathered three or four hundred assorted ships for his navy, with their merchant crews of three or four men each; and for an army, ten or twelve thousand men of the fyrd and house-carls. It would not have been worth while to mobilize a ship unless at least twenty fighting men could be put on board it, in addition to the crew who sailed it; so at least half the army must have been afloat, and perhaps much more of it. The remainder, spread out along the hundred and forty miles of coast from the Thames to the Isle of Wight, were clearly very thin on the ground; they could only be expected to report a landing, not to do much to oppose it. In all the centuries of attacks by Vikings, the English had never been able to stop them coming ashore; the invaders were free to choose their own place and approach it by night, so they always had the advantage of surprise. What the English had sometimes done, and the most they could hope to do again, was to watch and harass an invading army until their own had converged on the landing place, then stop it advancing inland. Given a favourable wind, a navy was simply the quickest way to assemble the army at whatever place the invaders chose to land – much quicker than marching it along the devious coastal tracks and ferrying it across the mouths of all the rivers.

That this was Harold's intention is confirmed by his choice of the Isle of Wight as a base. It was a matter of wind. The island was not in the middle of the vulnerable stretch of coast, it was right at the western end of it. But the Normans could only cross the Channel with a wind in the southerly quarter, and south-westerly winds in the Channel in summer are ten times more frequent than south-easterly winds. Thus the island, with a clear run eastward all the way to Beachy Head and Dover, gave the best chance of bearing down on invaders wherever they landed. From there, with any luck, the greater part of Harold's army might reach the landing place within a day and a night, to come ashore behind the invaders or on a neighbouring beach, and perhaps to beat up their ships where they lay at anchor or drawn up on the shore. It was perfectly logical strategy.

Such a great assembly of army and navy had never been made

before; yet there was no enemy in sight. At home on the land this was the busiest time of year, but down on the coast there was really nothing to do. At each of the posts on the cliffs and harbours, a couple of men on watch was as good as a hundred, and the rest could take it easy; and whenever the wind was northerly, everyone could relax and be perfectly certain no hostile fleet could come across the Channel. The fyrd was not bothered like later armies with drill; perhaps a few of the professional house-carls were sent from place to place to brush up the amateur's ideas of what to do in battle. The men seem not to have been paid, and nobody knows how their food was organized; but with a large proportion of thanes it was an army of gentry who knew how to take care of themselves. No doubt a good many brought their wives, and others found girl friends in neighbouring hamlets, as armies do. Probably some of them misbehaved. The idea of going away from home for a summer holiday had not yet entered anybody's mind, but it can never have been a hardship to spend a summer by the seaside, and one must suppose they made the best of it. There must have been a holiday atmosphere.

Of course it wore off. Any holiday can be too long. They began to be homesick, and to worry about the summer jobs they ought to be doing. As week after week went by and nothing happened, the feeling grew that nothing was ever going to happen. They started to grumble, as armies always grumble when they are bored, and to count the days to the end of their two months' service.

All that summer, Harold himself was in command of the fleet and the troops it carried. It is usually described as lying off the Isle of Wight, but that is another misunderstanding. Ships in those days were built to be hauled ashore on rollers, rather than lie at anchor in the open sea or even in a roadstead, for although one calls them ships they were really no more than large open boats. Their crews cooked their meals on land and slept in the ships under awnings. Perhaps a few were kept at sea for early warning, to signal by dipping their sails to watchers on the cliff-tops. But the hundreds of ships may be pictured lying in rows on the eastern beaches of the island; and at night, seen from the mainland shore, the light of uncountable camp fires.

Just across on that mainland shore is Chichester Harbour, and in it is Bosham, Harold's home. It was spelt Boseham then and is still pronounced Bozzam: and it is still a beautiful little place that any-one might cherish as a home, a village that covers a small peninsula among the tidal creeks; its outermost houses have their footings in the sea. It was already an ancient place when Harold lived there. Eight hundred years before, it had been a Roman settlement, and in the seventh century an Irish monk came sailing in and built himself a cell there, the first outpost of Christianity in that part of England.

The church where Harold worshipped is still intact, although the Normans extended it, and is still the parish church. Its chancel arch can be recognized, with a little imagination, in the Bayeux tapestry; its square tower was a landmark when Harold was a boy. A small girl is buried in its nave; she was the daughter of King Knut, who had a home there too. There is a water mill right on the edge of the sea, where no doubt there has been a mill since Harold's time. Yachts lie at their moorings now in the channel where his own ships lay, and at low tide small boats lie angled in the mud; the tapestry shows him with a hawk on his wrist and a small dog under his arm, wading out to his boat bare-legged in the shallow water for the fateful trip that ended at William's court.

It is not too much to hope he had time, in the summer of 1066, to rest in this timeless place. It was well placed as headquarters; messengers could reach him there from London or the Kent and Sussex coast, and boats could lie ready to take his orders to the men in the island – his own ship also, to lead them to the battle when the final message came. It also, like Horstede, had every homely quality. There all the old people had known him all his life. There he and his brothers had learned to swim and sail, hunt and fish, before the troubles of power had begun. Every building and every creek of the harbour must have held memories of them all. Now only three of the six were left: Svein the eldest was dead in disgrace, Tostig in exile, Wulfnoth the youngest imprisoned in Normandy. But Gyrth and Leofwine were with him in his present venture. There also his own three boys, now growing up, had learned the same lessons and had the same adventures, the next generation of the house of Godwin. There finally, one hopes, was their mother Edith Svanneshals to cheer him up and give him the comfort he must have sorely needed; for whatever his sceptical troops may have thought, he knew what was being prepared across the Channel.

Normandy

Spring

Very early in the spring, Duke William summoned a meeting of all the barons of Normandy in the castle of Lillebonne, which overlooks the estuary of the Seine, and told them he had decided to sail in force to England that very summer, to challenge Harold in battle and claim his just inheritance.

It is specially difficult to probe the motives of successful autocrats: their thoughts and wishes are not like anyone else's. Yet the Norman invasion was such a bizarre idea, so risky, so far beyond the bounds of military common sense, that one cannot just accept it as a fact. It has no satisfactory explanation outside the labyrinth of William's mind.

Nobody in northern Europe had ever tried to take a chivalric army across the sea. The Vikings, of course, had made far longer warlike voyages, but they never took horses with them. The Greeks of the Byzantine empire transported mounted troops, but their ships were bigger and more advanced in design. Both Vikings and Greeks could cope with contrary winds. A Mediterranean fleet had some ability to sail to windward, and it also had galleys designed to be rowed by slaves; and in a Viking war-fleet every soldier was also a life-long seaman, and the entire army could man the oars. But the fleet that William planned could neither be sailed to windward nor be rowed.

This is a point of such importance in his project that it needs to be elaborated a little. Some seamen would say that a ship of the Viking type – the only type that northern shipwrights could build – was able to make a point or two to windward. It is probably true of the Viking warships, but more doubtful of the broader cargo-ships that William perforce had to use to carry his horses and horsemen. And it is certainly not true of a whole fleet: a single ship with a good crew might make a little headway to windward, but it was quite impossible to tack a fleet of hundreds of ships, and nobody in the Middle Ages ever tried – they always waited, as William did, for a favourable wind. As for rowing, a sea-crossing of the length that William contemplated could only be made under oars with at least two shifts of oarsmen, which meant that practically everybody had to be able and willing to row: a fifty-foot ship, for example, had twenty-four oars and needed forty-eight oarsmen, and that left very little room for passengers. Moreover, if it was laden with horses it could not be rowed because there was no space for the sweep of the oars.

Yet William's intention meant transporting some thousands of horses and knights and a continental army of men who could not row – perhaps nobody in the world today has tried to row a twenty-four-oared ship in the waves of the open sea, but it would certainly take a lot of practice, and his project left no time for practice. It meant putting everything at the risk of a change of weather. Too much wind would have made havoc of a Norman fleet: it is a nightmare to think of a small open ship full of stallions in a storm at sea. Too little wind would have left it immovable, drifting with the tide, perhaps in full view from the shore of England. A change of direction might have driven it anywhere.

It was not a matter of straggling across, with each ship making what speed and course it could. That might have been good enough in a surprise invasion. But William knew, long before he sailed, that the coast of England was manned and Harold was waiting for him. He had to expect a devastating battle very soon after he landed. So it was essential for the fleet to stick together compactly and put the whole army quickly ashore in one place, men and horses fit and ready to fight.

Moreover, William could not cross the narrowest part of the Channel: opposite Dover, the coast belonged to the Count of Flanders and presumably – since he did not try it – he could not assemble his fleet and army in the count's domain. He assembled them in the River Dives, not far to the east of Caen, and from there it is a hundred miles to Beachy Head and the same to the Isle of Wight. With a wind of just the right strength in the right direction, a fleet like his might average five knots. It would take a day to load the ships and an ebb tide to get them out of the river; and after that day he needed at least another twenty-four hours of a gentle steady southerly breeze. Even now, such a long forecast is seldom reliable in the Channel, and in those days, weatherwise though they may have been, nobody could possibly have predicted such a spell of favourable wind.

The whole thing, therefore, was fraught with chances of disaster and depended entirely on luck – or as some of them believed, on an answer to their prayers; and no general trusts to luck, or entirely to prayer, unless he has a truly compelling reason.

I have suggested already that William's immediate feeling when he heard the news from England was of outraged pride, and I think that must have remained the prime cause of what he did. Nothing else seems credible. The old historians seldom looked for the motives of actions they recorded; when they tried, the one they most often chose was anger. Anger is a convenient explanation. Most motives are either virtuous or sinful; but anger, at least in their view, could be both, righteous in their friends and wicked in their adversaries. Their God was often vengeful and angry, it was something they understood; so they were content to say that William was angry. Yet nobody in his right mind can go on being angry very long. It causes an outburst, not a methodical course of action. William no doubt had moments of being very angry indeed, but eight months of meticulous preparation for the invasion of England could scarcely have been the product of anger alone.

Nor is greed for wealth or power an adequate explanation. One expects an autocrat to be greedy, and that might have driven William to other conquests, but not to the conquest of England. England was a rich prize, but there was endless scope for a conqueror on the mainland without the uncontrollable dangers of crossing the sea. To be King of France would have been a safer ambition. Napoleon and Hitler only attempted the conquest of England after conquering the rest of Europe, not before.

Again, William may have believed he was the chosen heir of England; but could he have hoped to retrieve that broken dream by conquest? They were two quite different things: to be welcomed and rule a willing people, or to come in force, to kill the reigning king and rule a sullen, resentful and rebellious people. In the beginning, he may have been too obtuse to see the difference: he lived among counties and duchies where might had always been right, and he did not know the English. But there were plenty of people in Normandy who did know the English and were able to warn him; and if he made that mistake, he let himself in for a lifetime of disillusion.

So one comes back to his personal pride, which I think is the only credible cause of the Norman invasion. At the beginning, it was a compelling motive: if he had done nothing, he would have damaged his own reputation and risked the loss of the power he already possessed. As things went on, this motive, unlike any others, must have become ever stronger: once having said he was going to England he could never back out, even when people told him, as many did, that the plan was impossibly dangerous. It has often been said he showed military genius, because he seemed sure of success from the very beginning, and won success in the end. I cannot bring myself to agree. Only a fool could have felt sure of success in this project, and William was not a fool. It would do him better justice to picture him, that spring and summer, keeping up a show of confidence to encourage the rest, but inwardly racked by uncertainty, haunted by a spectre of disaster, wishing there had been some other course, sometimes doubting that his claim was just or wise, yet persuading himself that God would support him – while all the time, the thing he had started led him farther and farther into deceit and danger.

Wounded pride is not a motive many people recognize in themselves, nor one they can use to win other people's support. To raise a big enough army William needed very wide support, in Normandy and outside it; and as soon as he made up his mind what to do he had to invent other motives, or allow them to be invented for him. In Normandy, among the barons and knights, invasion of England had to be made to seem a road to riches. Outside, it had to seem moral, the just punishment of a wicked man by the man he had wronged. Both these lines of argument led to claims that William knew were untrue – though in trying so hard to persuade other people, he may have persuaded himself.

Some time in February, he called a meeting of his closest allies and told them his decision. Among them were many men who became the great landlords of England, and some whose names run on through English history: his half-brothers Robert Count of Mortain and Odo Bishop of Bayeux; Roger of Beaumont, Walter Gifford, Hugh of Montfort, Roger of Montgomery, William of Warren, and the seneschal William FitzOsbern. These were the men, above all, whom he had to impress with his strength and determination. They were also men whose own position and power depended on his favour. Yet they were doubtful enough of his plan to say he should summon a wider council of all the barons and see what they had to say. Accordingly, a second much larger meeting was held – the meeting at Lillebonne.

Here William explained his grudge against Harold. He is reported to have made three complaints, and they are remarkable. The first was the murder of Alfred, King Edward's brother. This ancient crime, now almost thirty years in the past, was dragged out yet again; not only was Godwin accused of it once more, but also his sons. Nobody, in England or anywhere else, had ever suggested before that the sons had anything to do with it – they were all children at the time, and Harold was not much more than ten. But William now claimed Alfred as his kinsman and a friend of Normandy, and Harold as an accomplice in the murder, or a man who at least was stained by his father's guilt.

The second accusation was also from the distant past: that Godwin and his sons had driven Normans or Frenchmen out of England, especially Robert, the Archbishop of Canterbury – the man who had ignominiously fled when Godwin came home from exile in 1052. This was true enough, but was certainly not a crime; it was Godwin's doing rather than Harold's, and Harold in fact, since his father's death, had been tolerant of Edward's foreign friends.

The third accusation, more to the point, was that Harold was a perjurer who had broken an oath that was sworn on the relics of Norman saints, and usurped the kingdom that rightly belonged to William.

One has to think Harold had led a blameless life if this was the worst that William and his advisers could rake up against him. But the justice of William's claim was perhaps a minor point among the barons, who were well accustomed to the right of conquest. What interested them was whether the possible profits were worth the risks, and most of them firmly and loudly said they were not. They asked for time to think it over, and the meeting broke up into groups. The general feeling was that the feudal duty they owed to the Duke did not include fighting overseas, that the sea was too dangerous, England was too strong for Normandy, and the attempt would ruin them all. Where were the ships to come from, and who could possibly find enough oarsmen within a year? William Fitz-Osbern, the seneschal, tried to trick them. He listened to the arguments against the project, seemed to agree, and got the barons to appoint him as their spokesman. The meeting began again, and to their dismay he addressed the Duke in terms of servile loyalty: he promised he would himself provide sixty ships full of fighting men, and that everyone present would not only cross the sea with the Duke but would bring twice the number of men that duty demanded. There were angry shouts of disagreement which grew until nobody could hear himself speak, and the meeting ended in uproar.

This must have astonished and horrified William: it was not the kind of reception he was used to. He had miscalculated something. He knew the barons, he knew his feudal rights, and he knew from long experience just how far he could push them. There seems only one explanation: he had not understood until then how risky his project would be, and had put it to them with too much assurance and not enough persuasion.

William was no seaman, in spite of his Viking ancestry, nor were any of his close friends or followers. So far as is known he had never been to sea except when he visited Edward fifteen years before – and that was only a peaceful Channel crossing as a passenger. None of his interminable wars had taken him to sea, nor had the warlike sports that filled his leisure; seamanship was a servile trade in chivalric society. William had no experience of his own to judge the risks of the project, and it is unlikely he consulted a humble pilot before he consulted the barons - if he had, the poor man would only have dared to give him the answer he wanted.

Yet what could he do? Having announced his brave, defiant gesture, he could never withdraw it. No autocrat could answer the barons' clamour by saying, 'Ah well, perhaps you are right and I was wrong, it may be more dangerous than I thought.' He had to go on. He changed his tactics, summoned the barons one by one and spoke to each of them alone. Deprived of mutual support, not one of them was a match for him in a battle of wills, and each emerged from the interview having promised a certain number of knights and foot-soldiers – and having watched a clerk write down the promised figures in a ledger. Not many offered to come on the expedition in person, and possibly William preferred to leave them at home: most said they would send a son or some other relation in charge of their men. It is not recorded what inducement William offered them, except his own extreme displeasure if they refused. But there must at least have been hints at that stage of rich rewards in the form of estates in England.

The barons also perforce had to promise to build enough ships, and some of them from far inland must have wondered how on earth they were going to do it. But the problem of training oarsmen was dropped. It was obvious there would be no time, when the ships were ready, to teach some thousands of soldiers how to row. William assumed from beginning to end that the fleet would sail.

He also needed support from outside Normandy: even when the ledger was added up, the Normans could not or would not provide an army that was nearly strong enough. So he rode out on visits to the neighbouring counts and dukes, and to the King of France, to request them not to attack Normandy while he was away, and not to discourage knights and soldiers of their own domains from joining him. Other charges were made against Harold – one was adultery, which may have raised a smile among that adulterous nobility. Most of these other rulers probably thought William had a better claim than Harold. The right to rule, in their view, belonged to men of noble birth. William came of a line of rulers, though bastardy was a drawback, and Harold did not. The English way of choosing kings was little understood except in England. The witan's choice would not have meant much to them if they heard of it; and what they heard, of course, was the Norman story that Harold had seized the crown.

Nevertheless, they gave William a cautious reception. Most of them wanted to avoid the mistake of backing a loser, and preferred to wait and see what happened. The only one who promised to come in person with William was the same Count Eustace of Boulogne who had been bundled out of Dover so disrespectfully. He in fact had a better hereditary claim than William, since he was married to Edward's sister; and William, fearing perhaps that he might have big ideas, demanded he should leave his son in Normandy as a hostage.

On the other hand, the only one who made a positively hostile answer was a Count Conan of Brittany, who wished William good luck in his enterprise and added that he would certainly take the opportunity to seize Normandy, since he was the rightful heir to it and the Bastard was a usurper. Within a few days, the rash count was killed by somebody who smeared poison on his bridle, gloves and hunting horn. Some people blamed William, but poisoning was unlike him; a more charitable guess would be that it was done without his orders by someone who wanted to please him.

He also sent deputations as far as the courts of Denmark and Germany; and another, by far the most important of all, was despatched to Rome to seek the approval of the Pope. This embassy carried an entirely new argument in favour of William's plan, which bears the stamp of a subtler mind than his; and through it William's and Harold's rivalry became a pawn in political intrigues which were far beyond the provincial affairs of Normandy or England. The man behind these new ideas is thought to have been Lanfranc, who later became Archbishop of Canterbury, and at the beginning of 1066 was prior of the monastic college of Bec.

Lanfranc was Italian, and a highly respected scholar of logic and theology; also, like most high churchmen of his time, he was a politician, and not above using disreputable stratagems to promote what he thought was right. He had turned up in Normandy in his youthful wanderings nearly thirty years before, and lived there, sometimes in total seclusion, throughout the whole of William's rise to power. William had special reason to be grateful to him, because he was the man who persuaded the Pope to bless the marriage to Matilda. Lanfranc, on his side, knew William at least as a strong defender of the Norman church.

In all probability, this was the man who first pointed out the fundamental flaw in William's claim: Harold might be an unworthy man who had no right to be king, but that was no proof at all that William had any right to depose him. William's claim was too thin to impress a sophisticated judge. He had no witness of Edward's promise, and even Harold's had not been put in writing, which was already the usual custom for a solemn agreement. Both depended entirely on William's word. So far as anyone could know then – or can know now – he might have invented them both. As for his hereditary claim, it did not really exist. His great-aunt Emma had been the wife of Ethelred and Knut and mother of Edward, and that was his only remote relationship with the royal house of

England. To justify his project, William needed a totally different purpose.

It was probably Lanfranc too who conceived the new idea. The invasion should not be seen as a merely secular conquest; its highest aim should be, or appear to be, the reformation of the English church. It should become a crusade, a holy war to bring back an errant church to Rome. Lanfranc himself, or the Norman church as a body, was willing to bring accusations against the church of England.

It is always difficult to follow ancient sectarian arguments, and impossible now to judge whether the English church was really in need of reform. By modern standards, all churches then, and the Papacy itself, were full of corruption; the highest offices were often bought and sold, given as bribes or awarded to worldly men who were friends of kings. In that respect, the English church was certainly not the worst and may have been better than most. It was insular like the English themselves, and had tended to go its own way and show some independence of thought. It was perhaps too rich for its own good, especially in native works of art. Its Archbishop Stigand was specially open to attack because he had received his office while his Norman predecessor Robert was still alive, and because there was an irregularity in his confirmation by the Pope, and because he was guilty of pluralism in holding two sees, of Canterbury and Winchester. On the other hand, considering how remote it was from Rome, the church might have claimed it had been remarkably loyal. For two hundred years – if somewhat irregularly – it had collected and sent to Rome the offering known as Peter's Pence, and it had always encouraged Englishmen to make the pilgrimage. Perhaps its principal sin was merely to be different: much of its scholarship and all its pastoral work were in English instead of Latin, and it was easy for other churchmen to suspect that schisms and heresies were hidden by such a barbarous language. But finally, whatever was said against it, the fact remained that the English then were devoutly religious people and were satisfied on the whole that their church provided for their spiritual needs.

However, this was the reason for invasion that was submitted to the Pope. It was an afterthought in William's plan, and one can hardly believe it was anything but cynical – certainly in William, who was in no position to judge the English church, and probably in Lanfranc too. For it had ulterior motives. To William, it gave a chance of solving the problem of raising an army: he could promise land and booty to men who took part, but in a holy war the church could promise something more – salvation. To Lanfranc, it gave a chance to offer the Holy See an expansion of power it had been seeking in vain.

This is a tangled skein, but worth unravelling. The Papacy was just emerging from a time of scandalous disorder. Popes had been appointed by the Roman nobility, and later by the German emperor. Bribery had been rife, and the lives of popes had become suspiciously short. In 1046 there were three rival popes all at the same time, and the Emperor Henry III, on an expedition to Rome, dismissed all three of them and chose another. If anything was urgently in need of reformation it was this, and it had its ardent reformer in Cardinal Hildebrand, the most skilful politician in the Vatican.

In 1059, through Hildebrand's efforts, the election of popes had been taken away from secular politics and transferred to the College of Cardinals, and the Pope in office in 1066, Alexander II, was the first to be elected by the College – the second, seven years later, was Hildebrand himself. But in Hildebrand's eyes this was only half the battle. It was his lifelong belief not only that popes should not be elected by kings, but that kings should be elected by popes, or at least that their succession should be subject to papal approval.

Lanfranc could therefore ask for papal blessing of William's invasion and offer something of value in return: William's claim could be submitted to the judgement of the Pope. This would be the first time a pope had been asked to adjudicate a disputed royal succession, and would create a precedent of enormous importance to Hildebrand. Lanfranc was also in a unique position to get the judgement he wanted. He had been a close colleague of Hildebrand: they had battled together against a powerful heresy that denied Transsubstantiation. And the present Pope, as it happened, had once been his student at Bec.

With this brief, the embassy rode to Rome. Lanfranc did not go in person; the case was entrusted to the Archdeacon of Lisieux. In Rome, some time in the spring, Harold's and William's rights were solemnly debated in the papal court, without the slightest reference to the facts. Harold was not represented. It is not recorded whether he was invited to send an advocate, but it is very unlikely. To ride from Rome to Bosham and back again to Rome suggests a month on the road, and nobody was prepared to waste as much time as that. If he had been invited, he and the witan would certainly have answered, quite correctly, that the choice of a King of England had nothing to do with the Pope. The court was divided; perhaps somebody pointed out that they were only hearing one side of the argument. But with Hildebrand, the archdeacon and Lanfranc's ex-student on that side and nobody on the other, the result was not hard to foretell. The Pope accepted that William's purpose was to reform the church, he sent his blessing on this holy endeavour, a papal banner to carry into battle, and a ring for William to wear on the expedition which contained a relic of St Peter himself. There was one condition: it was understood that William would hold England as a vassal of the Pope. William had not the least intention in the world of doing anything of the sort; but he accepted the ring and the banner and said nothing. And those, as things turned out, were the most powerful weapons he took to England.

With that triumphant sophism, things began to move quickly. Volunteers came pouring into Normandy, knights and their attendants, foot soldiers alone and in bands, from every county from Flanders to Aquitaine, from the royal demesne of France, and especially from Brittany, which was full of impoverished landless knights. By this time it was widely known that William was offering landed estates in England to his leaders and booty for everyone; while to anyone who died in the holy cause, the church would offer absolution. A fortune if they succeeded or heaven if they failed: this call has attracted armies all through history.

Yet it was not the kind of army William had wanted. Nothing had worked out quite as he intended. Looking back at these events one can hardly blame him, except for being the kind of man his birth and position had made him – a man too proud and too powerful to be able to admit he was wrong. It seems that he made two mistakes, both human and understandable. He clung too long to the dream that when he had landed in England and beaten Harold in battle, the English would welcome him. And he did not know, until it was too late to draw back, how risky his project was. So he made his proposal, and only then found the barons would not support him and he could not raise enough men.

To buy their support and attract volunteers, he began to promise estates in England, committing himself to seize the most precious possession of Englishmen, their land. So he destroyed whatever hope he had had of ruling willing people. His claim as the rightful heir had become a punitive expedition – and not against Harold only, but against the English. Finally, to bring more men, he had connived in deceiving the Pope, which may have weighed on his conscience more than anything, and saddled himself with a promise he knew he would break. At the end of it all, he did not have an army of loyal Norman lieges: two-thirds of it were miscellaneous foreign mercenaries, hard to control and impossible to trust, who did not know or care about the justice of his cause but were only intent on booty.

Norway

Summer

While all this hectic activity was going on in Normandy, nothing
was happening in England – or so one must suppose, because there
is no report of any event from June to September, and the situation
at the end of that time was the same as it had been at the beginning.
Harold was waiting with the whole of his fleet and most of his army
in the Isle of Wight, and the rest of the army was scattered along the
coast of Kent and Sussex. Without taking sides one can make com-
parisons: compared with the cunning in Normandy, there seems an
air of pastoral innocence in the English scene. Perhaps it was too
innocent. Harold has been blamed for many things, and one of them
is over-confidence. He knew what William was doing, and seemed
to be confident he could stop him.

He knew because William was making no secret of it. People then
had hardly started to think of secrecy as an advantage in war; on
the contrary, they challenged their enemies, boasted about their
strength and displayed it if they could. People knew about William's
plans all over Europe, and Harold had fought with William's army
against the Bretons only two years before. Also, he had spies.

Norman stories say one of them was caught observing William's army, and rather than punish him William sent him back to England with two defiant messages. The first was that Harold need not waste his money paying spies, because William would be in England before the year was out to show him the strength of the Norman army. The second was a strange taunt: that William had promised to give away all Harold's possessions, but Harold was too weak to promise any of William's possessions.

Presumably, therefore, Harold not only knew William was coming but knew the kind of troops he was bringing; and critics specially blame him for being content with an army of foot-soldiers and not organizing a mounted army like William's, or even a corps of archers.

It is a safe guess that the Normans' weapons were a favourite topic of conversation at Bosham that summer, between Harold and his brothers, and the captains of the house-carls, and any important people who happened to call: Harold, the author of the *Vita Aedwardi* said, always discussed his plans with anyone he trusted. It is also safe to assume the problem looked rather less straightforward then than it does in the light of after-knowledge. Bows and arrows in particular were important weapons: forerunners of guns, they had much longer range than the spears and stones and weighted sticks the English possessed to throw at their enemies. On the face of it, it looks a simple matter to equip a few thousand men with bows. But bows in England were aristocratic sporting weapons, used for shooting deer not human enemies, and archery was a strictly guarded mystique. For a long time past, the nobles had been fanatically jealous of their hunting rights, and if a poor man owned a bow he labelled himself a poacher. No common soldier in the fyrd would be any good at archery, or admit it if he was; the training would have to start from scratch. Could aristocrats be persuaded or compelled to put this privileged weapon into the army's hands? Would they give their cherished bows, or lend their bowmakers? A very deep-rooted prejudice had to be overcome.

A mounted army was even more difficult – not just a matter of training men but horses too. The stallions of Norman knights were bred and broken for fighting, and selective breeding had probably made them much bigger than English horses, which were like the half-wild shaggy ponies that are still living in some of the English forests. (It is said a lot of horseshoes were found in the nineteenth century around the battlefield of Stamford Bridge, where Harold fought the Norsemen that September, and they were all so small they would have fitted donkeys.) Moreover, every man's horse was his own. It was worth money – and most men are fond of their horses. A Norman knight was obliged by his feudal duty to ride his horse into battle, but an English thane was not, and he would have needed a lot of persuading. So would his horse.

Perhaps the English, and the King himself, were too complacent. But both these new kinds of fighting needed instruction and practice, and both also needed a fundamental change in English habits of mind. Both needed time – but the threat was imminent. A winter might have been spent on new ideas, but for the moment the army had to make the best of what it had. Evidently, it was not much alarmed by the threat of new weapons. Against arrows, it had wooden shields, and against horsemen, by most remarkable reasoning or instinct, it had already thought of the means of defence that was still in use seven hundred and fifty years later at Waterloo: to stand in close ranks with spears pointing up and outward – it was bayonets at Waterloo – which made a frieze of spikes no horse was ever trained to charge.

Its confidence was not entirely ill-founded. Events were to prove that Harold's defence was adequate against the threat he knew. But he knew only half the threat. He knew what William was doing, but so far as one can tell he had no idea what his brother Tostig was doing.

When Tostig disappeared to the north in May, he did not stay long with Malcolm King of Scots; he sailed across to Oslofjord in Norway and met the Norwegian King whose name was Harald (spelt with two a's) and whose nickname was Hardrada. So he brought into the English drama the most flamboyant of all its characters – a man who was fifty years old in 1066, who had first been wounded in battle when he was fifteen, and who had been fighting battles at every possible opportunity ever since.

This part of the story is not in English or Norman chronicles, but in the book called Heimskringla, or the Lives of the Norse Kings, which was written by the Icelandic poet and historian Snorri Sturlasson about the year 1230. It was rather ancient history when he wrote it, and it is easy to find mistakes in the parts of it that are English rather than Norse. But the Icelanders of that era had a passion for history, and did their best to separate fact and legend; and Snorri compiled, from earlier sagas, a more complete and less openly prejudiced biography of the Norwegian king than anyone wrote of any of the others. It is a very surprising story, and perhaps it makes Harald a little larger than life, but there is no reason to think it is not substantially true.

It was an odd custom that Norsemen gave their nobles nicknames or epithets. Most of them were straightforward; among the kings were Harald Fairhair, Erik Blood-axe, Halvdan the Black, Olav the Peaceful, Olav the Fat, Magnus Barefoot, Hakon Broadshoulder and Magnus the Good. But Hardrada is one of the composite words that are common in Old Norse and cannot be neatly translated. In modern Norwegian it would be spelt Hårdråde and pronounced Hordrorde: hård means hard and råde means council. But Hard in Council is a poor rendering of what must have been a pithy, appropriate nickname. Perhaps Hard Bargainer is somewhere near the sense of it, and perhaps the nearest single words that might have made nicknames are Ruthless, Tough or Stubborn.

Any of those would have suited King Harald pretty well. Although he lived when the peak of Viking enterprise was past, he was typical of the Vikings' unique poetic barbarity. He once said of himself, in verse, that he had eight accomplishments: he could shoe a horse, ride, swim, ski, shoot, throw javelins, play the harp and compose poetry. Snorri adds to this that he was enormously tall and broad, had very large hands and feet and a very loud voice, fair hair and beard and a long moustache, and one eyebrow higher than the other. He was nominally a Christian, although it was less than half a century since Norway had been forcibly converted by his predecessors; but he managed to have two wives, apparently of equal status, and to live a life in which the principal pleasures were fighting, duplicity and hoarding gold. He was unpopular among his own people because his cruelty was dishonest and capricious, but he was shrewd enough to keep himself alive and on top in his dangerous world. It was said he had never run away from battle, and he had a great reputation for cunning stratagems to get himself out of tight corners.

In the battle when he was fifteen, which was in 1030, he was on the losing side. He was fighting for his half-brother King Olav against the Norwegians themselves, who were in revolt. Olav was killed (he was canonized in the thirteenth century on account of miracles recorded at his tomb) and consequently Harald had to hide in forests until his wounds were healed and then escape from the country. He fled by the old-established Viking route that led through the rivers of Russia all the way from the Baltic to the Black Sea; and after a year or two in the army of the King of Novgorod he reached Constantinople, and enrolled in the forces of the Byzantine Empress Zoë.

A large part of the army of the Byzantine Empire in that era was formed of adventurers who had come all the way from Scandinavia – a journey which in itself took over a year. Harald quickly rose to be captain of it. While he was still a very young man, he was leading the Empress's troops in attacking and sacking towns in North Africa and Sicily, and Snorri's story is full of relish, half in awe and half in admiration, for the swindles and trickery he used to discredit his rivals, and the successful rapine and plunder he used to assemble a following of his own. All the major Mediterranean towns were proof against direct attacks or sieges, but none against Harald's cunning. At one in Sicily, camped outside the impregnable walls, he noticed that small birds were nesting in the thatch of the houses and flying out by day to the woods for food. He set men to catch the birds, bind chips of fir in their backs, pour melted wax and brimstone on the fir and set it on fire. 'As soon as they were freed, the birds flew back to the town to seek their young in the nests. Although each bird carried only a little burden of fire, each set light to the thatch and soon the whole town was in flames.'

Besieging another town, Harald fell sick and conceived the idea of staging his own funeral. His men told the townspeople their leader was dead, and begged for his Christian burial in one of the churches within the walls. There was great competition among the priests to accept the body, because they expected rich offerings from the Norsemen. All the priests came out of the town to form a procession, and the Norsemen marched mournfully in with them, bearing a coffin; and inside the gates, dropped the coffin and blew a war blast on their horns. 'The monks and other priests who had striven to be the first to receive the corpse now struggled to get away from the Norsemen, who slew everyone round them, clerk or layman, ravaged the town, slaughtered the men, robbed all the churches and loaded themselves with booty.'

These were the kind of deeds that delighted Norsemen, and Harald became a hero among them. He also became, it was said, the richest Norseman there had ever been, and he sent his plunder over the years to safe keeping with his friend the King of Novgorod. After ten years or so in the east he thought it was time to go home; and then there was trouble. The Empress accused him of swindling over the booty: Norse rumour said she wanted him as a husband, although she already had one – the second of three in her lifetime. Harald, on the other hand, wanted a girl named Maria who was her niece. The Empress put him in prison. His saintly and dead half-brother Olav appeared in the night to a woman he had miraculously cured, and told her to rescue Harald – which she did by letting down ropes from the prison roof. He rounded up his followers, personally put out the eyes of the Empress's husband in a street of the city, abducted Maria and escaped by rowing a galley over a defensive chain that was stretched across the Golden Gate to stop him. He sent Maria home with an offensive message to the Empress and set sail across the Black Sea and up the river Dnieper to Novgorod, where he collected his treasures and married the King's daughter Elizabeth.

He came back to Norway in 1042, the year when Edward came to the throne in England. The country was ruled by King Olav's son, Magnus the Good, but Harald was so rich and had such a fearsome reputation that Magnus had to give him half the kingdom, and when Magnus died five years later, Harald succeeded to it all. Magnus had also been King of Denmark, but the Danes refused to have Harald and chose Swein Ulfson, who was son of the Danish earl Ulf who had befriended Godwin as a boy, and was thus a nephew of King Knut and first cousin of Harold of England and Tostig. Thereafter, Harald spent no less than fifteen years, summer after summer, in attacking, ravaging and burning Denmark and trying to kill or overthrow King Swein.

Nobody but a Norseman could have lived such a life in that era. The fact was that Norsemen (or Vikings, the words are almost synonymous) had always shown a dual character. They lived as simple farmers and were capable of lawful government, either at home or in the countries where they settled on their Viking expeditions; but they also found an ecstatic joy in bloodshed. The Normans and English were largely of Norse descent, but on the whole they represented the settled part of the Norseman's nature. Harald was a pure example of the other part. His incessant battles were not mainly a means to political ends, or even a means of enriching himself. They were fought for the sheer delight of fighting.

The word berserk has survived from the Norseman's language. A man who went berserk was seized by a battle-madness far beyond courage: he killed and killed, without mercy, reason or fear, and did not stop until there was nobody left to kill, or until he fell dead himself. Such berserkers were the heroes of the Norsemen. Norse poetry glories in the feats of men who went mad in battle, men who were called in the awkward composite words weapon-strong, steel-grim, sword-eager, war-happy, raven-feeders. Its images are of the clutch of death, the clash of steel, the sword that bites the shields, the cloven skulls, the thin smile of the battle-axe, the severed limbs, the blood, the scattered brains, and always the ravens, wolves or eagles that feast on corpses. It revels in destruction, the burning of homes, the tears of women, the rape and plundering.

This poetry has no greater hero than Harald. Scores of verses still exist to praise his bestiality:

'Harald, you ravaged all Zealand, you gave the helmets
Hard work to bear; the shields were burst asunder.
Fiercely the fires burned in the farms of Roskilde:
The warrior king made the ruined houses glow.
The countrymen lay fallen: Hel the Goddess of Death
Had robbed them of their freedom. Those who lived
Fled, bent with anguish, to the forests.
The fairest women were seized: the lock held the maiden's body.
You sent before you many unwilling women to the ships:
The fair-skinned bore the chains.
The grey eagle's keen claws, O King, you dyed in blood,
The wolf was always fed before you went homeward.'

One such poem has the running refrain:

'May the soul of mighty Harald
Abide eternally with Christ.'

Harald, in one word, was berserk; the most celebrated, feared
and admired berserker of that century. Yet in 1063 he had to admit
he had failed in Denmark: fifteen years of war had not subdued the
Danes. At last, he made a pact with King Swein. When Tostig
came into Oslofjord in 1066, Harald was still smarting from this
ignominy, and for the first time in his life had passed two summers
with nobody to fight, except a few of his own subjects who had
raised a feeble revolt.

For poor Tostig, the voyage to see this terrible man was a final hope.
Whether or not he was wholly sane, he was certainly obsessed
beyond all reason by his resentment and his feeling of persecution.
He did not care in the least who ruled England, whether it was well
or badly governed, prosperous or wholly ravaged by war, independent or the slave-dominion of a foreign king – if only he could
achieve his impossible aim of being accepted again in the earldom
that had risked a civil war to get rid of him. He had been on a
begging mission to every possible person who had the power to
help him – to the Count of Flanders, King Swein of Denmark, Duke
William of Normandy and King Malcolm of the Scots – and he had
tried to fight his way back into England all alone. Everyone had re-

jected him, not unkindly but very firmly. Probably all the four rulers, and certainly the King of Denmark and the Count of Flanders, had been willing to give him a home and even a place of honour. But not one of them had been willing to fight against England on his behalf; and for four such disparate men to have reached the same decision, his claims must have been quite obviously hopeless.

The accounts of Tostig's voyages are rather confused, and some people have doubted if there was time in 1066 for him to have made them all. I think there was, with one unimportant exception. According to Snorri, he went first from Flanders to Denmark to ask for the help of King Swein – who offered him an earldom in Denmark but said he had no quarrel with Harold of England. It is the Norman chroniclers who say he went to Normandy. The Anglo-Saxon Chronicle fixes the date of his abortive attack soon after the comet, which makes it early in May. Snorri says he went to Norway in the spring, then back to Flanders to collect some followers he had left there; and he was certainly in Scotland again in August.

It is a busy six months, but it is quite feasible: Denmark in February, Normandy in April, the Isle of Wight and then Scotland in May and Norway at the beginning of June – which an Icelander might reasonably call the spring. The main doubt is that Snorri insists it was Tostig who first proposed to King Harald Hardrada that he should make an attack on England – and Harald's fleet was undoubtedly ready to do so by early August. It seems little time at first glance – not more than two months – for Harald to have assembled a fleet and an army, and the doubters have deduced that he had already decided to do it and started his preparations before Tostig arrived on the scene.

But this also I think is quite possible. Harald's problem in Norway was nothing compared with William's in Normandy. No Viking king had to justify an aggressive war; no cover-story had to be devised; no barons had to be bribed or neighbours to be persuaded – and least of all would Harald have cared what the Pope would think about it. On the contrary, Norway had plenty of warriors frustrated by two summers without a battle, longing for the ecstasy of a fight, itching for plunder, not even needing orders but only an invitation, a 'bidding', to come and join a promising expedition. Moreover the Norsemen, unlike the Normans or the English, were truly seafaring people and their fleet already existed, designed for war and ocean voyages, and lying with nothing to do among the western fjords. Harald had many celebrated ships that had often fought in Denmark: one for example that was modelled on the most famous of all Viking warships, the Long Serpent of his predecessor Olav Trygvasson, which was propelled by thirty-six pairs of oars and carried at least two hundred and fifty men. Such a ship, with three shifts or watches and seventy-two oarsmen in each, could keep up a speed of eight or even ten knots for a very long time, and easily cross the North Sea in summer in any direction of wind.

Harald could therefore be ready at very short notice to make an expedition. Indeed, the whole thing has the air of a last-minute idea: August is the end of the summer in the northern seas, and if it had been a long-term project he would certainly have started earlier in the season. Moreover Snorri's story of the meeting of Harald and Tostig is so circumstantial that one feels compelled to believe it. He reports their discussion verbatim, and although the words are obviously his own the trend of the argument is wonderfully convincing.

He does not say how Tostig sailed to Norway, or how he found King Harald; but the obvious way from Scotland was first to go to the Orkney Islands, which were a Norse possession ruled by an earl named Torfinn. Ships often crossed between Norway and Orkney in the summer; Torfinn would certainly know where the King could be found – it might have been anywhere south of Trondheim, which was his capital – and could very likely offer a better ship than Tostig's which was going that way.

When they met, Tostig told the King about his journeys and said he wanted help to 'get his realm'. Harald replied that Norsemen would not want to go to England and make war there when it already had an English king. He added significantly: 'People say the English are not entirely to be trusted.'

Tostig changed his tactics. 'I have heard people say in England,' he said, 'that your predecessor King Magnus sent an embassy to

King Edward in England. He claimed he had a sworn agreement with Harthaknut, through which he should have inherited not only Denmark but England too.* Is it true that he had a right to England?'

'If he had a right to it, why did he not possess it?' Harald said.

'Why did you not possess Denmark,' Tostig replied, 'just as Magnus possessed it?'

The King answered irritably: 'The Danes have nothing to boast about against us Norsemen. Many a hole we burned there among your kinsmen.'

'If you will not tell me, I will tell you,' Tostig said. 'King Magnus took Denmark into his possession because all the nobles of the country helped him. You did not get it because the nobles were against you. Likewise Magnus did not fight for England because the English wanted Edward for their king. But if *you* want to win England I can fix it so that most of the nobles will be your friends and helpers. Compared with my brother Harold I lack nothing except the name of King. Everyone knows no warrior to compare with you has ever been born in Norway. It seems strange to me that you would fight fifteen years to get Denmark, but you will not have England which is lying ready for you to take.'

So Tostig had begun, as one might expect, by asking for help to win the crown of England for himself; and when that was about to be refused, he had changed his tune and offered his help to Harald, so that Harald would become King of England and Tostig presumably would get his old earldom as a reward. He could not have put his case more shrewdly: it appealed equally to Harald's ambition and greed, to his chagrin at the Danish failure, and to his longing for another adventure. But Tostig's promise to bring the nobles of England to Harald's side was of course a sheer delusion. Six months before, when Tostig was exiled, not one of the nobles spoke up for him although he had Edward's support: now Edward was dead, they were even less likely to do so – and least likely of all to welcome a berserk Norseman as King. In fact, he had not a

---

* This claim is not mentioned in English chronicles, but there was probably some truth in it: in the early part of his reign, Edward assembled a fleet at Sandwich because King Magnus was expected to attack.

single influential friend in the country except perhaps his sister the widowed queen. No doubt it was this pathetic gap between Tostig's belief and the sad reality that had made all the other rulers turn him down. They all knew pretty well what was happening in England. But Harald Hardrada did not. Norway was almost completely cut off from western Europe. It may have been years since any reliable informant had come from England, Normandy or Flanders to Harald's court; and Denmark was implacably hostile. So Harald Hardrada, unlike the other rulers, knew nothing of English affairs; and unlike them, he was deceived by Tostig's unbalanced and entirely untrue belief. In him, there is no need to look for subtle motives: he was a far more primitive man than either William or Harold of England. He was tempted. He wanted the excitement of a new expedition; he wanted another rousing battle before he was too old; he wanted England. Also, he very possibly needed a popular foreign war to divert the energy of his own rebellious people.

Snorri says that Harald and Tostig talked long and often together, and they agreed: Harald would prepare his fleet and army, Tostig would go back to Flanders and fetch some friends he had left there, and they would meet again in Scotland.

But I think this final voyage of Tostig's must be one of Snorri's minor mistakes. If Tostig went back to Flanders at that moment he would have had to do it in both directions without touching either of the hostile coasts of Denmark or England – a long and risky voyage, and a feat of navigation not even a Viking would have tried with confidence. With the luckiest possible winds it might have been done in three weeks, but it might have taken three months; and if he was late for the meeting in Scotland, he would lose everything. It is much more likely he went straight back to Scotland and rounded up whatever followers he had left at Malcolm's court.

Harald sent out his bidding all through Norway, and called out a levy on half the people: one cannot know precisely what that meant, except that he had called a levy on all the people for the Danish wars, which suggests that only enthusiasts were expected to volunteer for England. At all events, plenty of men responded, and assembled with the ships at the island of Solund, which is off the mouth of Sognefjord in the west of Norway. There was great discussion of their prospects. Some recalled Harald's deeds in the past and were sure that nothing was impossible. Others had ominous dreams. One dreamed he saw a bird on the stem of each ship, and every bird was an eagle or a raven. Another dreamed he saw the English army, and it was led by a huge troll woman riding on a wolf which had a man's body in its jaws and blood running out of the corners of its mouth; and when it had eaten the man, the woman threw it more and it ate them all.

Harald made his family dispositions. He had two wives, two daughters and two sons. He appointed one son, Magnus, to rule Norway while he was away. The other, Olav, was to come with him; and so was the elder of his wives, Elizabeth of Novgorod, and his daughters Maria and Ingegerd.

Then he went to Trondheim, where he unlocked the shrine of King Olav and cut his hair and nails, which were still growing, owing to his sanctity, thirty-five years after his death. He threw the key of the shrine into the neighbouring River Nid; and early in August, he sailed to join his ships.

North Wind

◆━━━◆━━━◆

August 10 - September 12

At just the same time, the beginning of August, the last of Duke William's ships were ready and were sailing into the harbour he had appointed, the mouth of the river Dives. Compared with Harald Hardrada's, the fleet was improvised and unseamanlike; for all the Norsemen were seamen from their childhood up, and most of the Normans were not.

The difference was caused by the nature of their seas. The coasts of Scandinavia have thousands of miles of sheltered tideless waterways which for centuries past had been a natural thoroughfare; when Norsemen went anywhere, they went by boat. But the coast of Normandy is the opposite. It has hardly any sheltered water. In the open sea, off the points of land, there are five-knot tidal streams, and the range between high and low water goes up to forty feet. There are very few harbours, and most of them are the mouths of rivers like the Dives, where the tides pour in and out and small ships can only go out on the ebb and come in again on the flood. Any Norman who put to sea, even to catch a few fish, had to stay there exposed to the weather until the tide was right to go in again, and avoid being carried away by it.

So, in the hundred and fifty years since their Viking ancestors landed, the Normans had lost the habit of using the sea. In normal times there were not many ships in the country, and where there are not many ships there are not many shipbuilders. The barons, ordered to build a fleet in six months, must desperately have rounded up every woodman and carpenter in the country and installed them on the nearest river banks with orders to get on with the job, whether or not they had ever built a ship or a boat in their lives.

The Bayeux tapestry shows them doing it. Men with axes lop off the branches of trees. Another, with an axe of a different shape, has propped up a pole against a forked post and is standing astride it, hewing it down to a plank: stacks of poles and finished planks are lying beside him. Other men, using small adzes, are working on ships that are already planked: they might be shaping the frames to fit inside the planking. Finally others, bare-legged, are hauling the ships to the water. The ships are loaded with spears and axes, the chain-mail, swords and helmets of knights and some barrels of wine; and then in the tapestry they are shown at sea.

These pictures of ships are doubly marvellous: apart from their artistry, no others within the next four hundred years are so satisfactory to a seaman's eye. It would be stupid to hunt for too much technical detail in a medieval work of art, especially an embroidery. But from the tapestry one can learn a very useful amount about the fleet the barons built for William.

They were ships of the old Norse type, double-ended with high curved stems and sternposts, mostly decorated with dragons' heads and tails. This was the only kind of ship that northern shipwrights learned to build before the fourteenth century, though Mediterranean builders were far in advance of them. In structure it was as simple as a ship can be: it could be beautifully built, or it could be knocked together very quickly. A small boat of this design needed only three planks a side; the larger Norse ships had sixteen: in the largest shown in the tapestry, five or six planks are visible above the waterline. Although they were economical in labour, they were prodigiously wasteful in timber. No early medieval woodman, before the pit-saw was invented, could make more than two planks from a log: he split it and flattened each half. A ship of moderate size needed twenty large trees for its planking, keel and stems.

The only ship in the tapestry which is shown with oars is the one that took Harold to Normandy – or rather to Ponthieu – in 1064. In William's fleet at sea, all the ships have masts and sails, and none is being rowed: one is being poled ashore in shallow water, while the crew lower the mast and horses jump overboard. About half of them have tholes or oar-holes, which show they were built to be rowed. The larger ones are designed for either ten or twelve pairs of oars which, by comparison with Viking ships, suggests a length overall of forty-five to fifty-five feet. One, the largest of all, which has no dragon's head or decoration, has sixteen tholes, the same number as the Gokstad ship preserved in Oslo, which is seventy-six-and-a-half feet long. But the smallest are very small: some are full up with four or five men in them, and one of the carpenters who has nearly finished a ship is represented – with artistic licence – standing astride it with his feet on the ground on each side.

One might suppose the number of tholes is only arbitrary, chosen to fit the design or even the needlework. But there is one ship quite different from all the rest: the ship that brought Harold back from Normandy in 1064 has twenty tholes, plus a space amidships where the gunwales are lower and there are no tholes – the space that would be left in a ship designed to be rowed without lowering the mast. This is a much bigger ship than any in William's fleet: it would have been nearly a hundred feet in length, and it demonstrates that the designer was being careful about this detail of his ships.

Without stretching this artistic evidence too far, one may say that William's fleet had ships that varied in size from boats that might be called sailing dinghies now, up to the single ship of seventy-six feet, with a main force of the forty-five to fifty-five footers. These, I surmise, were built by a kind of mass-production: to build a large number of ships with rather unskilled labour, it would be sensible to produce enough sets of standard moulds and distribute them round the temporary shipyards. With their ten or twelve pairs of oars, they were small by Viking standards – about half the size of the commonest kind of Viking warship, which had twenty-four pairs, and a third of the size of Harald Hardrada's largest, which with its thirty-six pairs was probably a hundred and sixty feet long.

In the tapestry, all the larger ships except two are laden with horses: the seventy-six footer has ten in it and eight men, some of whom are chatting together with the supercilious but nervous expressions one might expect in knights who had put to sea. The two ships without horses have shields stowed along the gunwales, which was the Vikings' practice in their warships – though not, as a rule, at sea but only as a decoration when they were entering harbour. One of these is the Duke's own ship, distinguished by a lantern and a cross at the masthead, the leopard of Normandy on the prow and the figure of a boy on the sternpost blowing a horn. It has no visible tholes, but carries twelve shields a side; so one may suppose the Duke's ship was another with twelve pairs of oars and a length of forty-five to fifty-five feet.

These ships with shields no doubt represent the proportion which carried oarsmen and were prepared to fight at sea if they had to. The rest are the transports with the troops and cargo and especially the horses, and these could not be rowed on the crossing: firstly because the horses left no room for the sweep of oars, and secondly because there were not enough men who could row.

The number of ships that William assembled is an enigma. Figures in early accounts range from six hundred and ninety-six to eleven thousand. The barons' promises, added together, come to about eight hundred and fifty; but of course those were only promises. It has been surmised that the lower figures refer to the larger ships, and the higher ones include all the small boats. But all through history, the numbers of ships and men in navies and armies have been vastly exaggerated, and I think that even the lowest figure is far too high. Harold's fleet, which I have estimated at four hundred, was the largest there had ever been in England. Harald Hardrada's is said by Snorri to have had two hundred ships, with small boats and supply ships in addition, and he implies that this number is almost incredibly large, even by Viking standards. To build six hundred and ninety-six ships meant felling, transporting and converting something like twelve or fifteen thousand good-sized forest trees.

The size of the fleet that William needed depended, of course, on the size of his army, and that is also uncertain. Before Hastings he sent a message to Robert FitzWimark claiming he had sixty thousand men and would still have been willing to attack if he had only had ten thousand. Modern opinion (to which I shall return) is that this was a military bluff and he did in fact have about ten thousand, and perhaps three thousand horses. In the tapestry, the number of men and horses in each ship is a matter of artistic design; but it would be common sense to think that a fifty-foot ship could carry sixty men, or perhaps half the number of men and ten horses. Unlike later armies, William's had no heavy equipment – no ammunition but arrows, no weapons they could not carry, no more than a couple of days' supply of food. The horses were by far the bulkiest cargo, and the only heavy things were their barrels of wine and the timber for two or three ready-made forts. On this basis, three hundred and fifty ships would have been plenty – three hundred transports each with ten horses and thirty men, and fifty ships without cargo which might have used oars if an enemy had been sighted.

None of this argument, of course, is an adverse criticism of William or his army: it is not a sin to be unseamanlike. On the contrary, it magnifies their achievement: William's will-power in creating a fleet, even a second-class fleet, in a country that knew so little about it, and the soldiers' courage in putting to sea.

The river Dives has silted up and runs morosely now through miles of meadows which are often flooded, and winds to the sea among enormous sand-banks; but then it made a spacious tidal roadstead. Even three hundred and fifty ships would have made a brave enough sight drawn up on the muddy banks with an army of chivalry encamped around them in the summer sun. Knights already delighted in colour and glittering metal, carried banners of their own design and shields painted with devices that proclaimed who they were and where they came from. There is an idyllic description of the scene, written by the Duke's chaplain William of Poitiers, who was an excessively sycophantic man: 'The Duke made generous provision, for his own knights and for those from foreign parts. Such was his moderation and prudence that he utterly forbade pillage, and provided for fifty thousand soldiers at his own expense. The flocks and herds of the peasantry pastured unharmed throughout the province. The crops waited undisturbed for the sickle without being trampled by the pride of the knights or ravaged by the greed of the plunderers. A weak and unarmed man, watching the swarm of soldiers without fear, might follow his horse singing wherever he would . . . In every deliberation, all men deferred to the prudent wisdom of the Duke, as if the Divine Intelligence had indicated to him what ought to be done and what ought to be avoided. "God gives wisdom to the pious", one skilled in divinity has said, and the Duke had acted piously since his childhood; so all obeyed him in whatsoever he ordered, unless they were reluctantly forced to admit an overriding necessity.'

Nevertheless the fleet and the army were stuck in the river until the wind came from the south; and on 10 August it began to blow from the north.

In England, Harold had nobody to sing extravagant praises, but he had the same problem that William solved so graciously. His army had been where it was for over two months, and it had eaten the countryside bare. Not that it lived by plunder; but no part of England could support an extra ten thousand men. Food was having to come from farther and farther afield, brought on pack-animals along the country tracks. Prices no doubt were rising, and Harold's resources as king were not unlimited. The strains on his organization were growing serious.

What was worse, perhaps, the fyrd had already finished the two months' service it owed for 1066. Not many of these men, not even the travelled thanes, had ever in their lives been so long away from their villages. Not many had heard a word of news from home:

who, for example, would have come to search for Ulfer to tell him what was happening in Horstede? At home in their villages, they were isolated from the world outside: and outside, they were utterly isolated from their villages. Any man would have worried, about his wife and children, an ageing parent perhaps, the harvest, the animals, the thousand and one odd jobs of a farmer's life, and all the trivialities of home. He would have imagined disaster, and passionately longed to go back. Especially he would have feared the winter: in August and September, certain work had to be done – logs cut, meat salted down, fish dried, corn ground, wool woven – or the winter could easily turn to fatal cold and famine.

Day after day that August, the northerly wind continued. It made them safer, but also more restless. All summer they had been told the Normans were coming and they had not come; with such a wind they certainly could not come: the equinox was only a month away, and then the winter when no invader had ever come. The summer had all been wasted, and every day of the off-shore breeze was another waste of time, another day when the urgent work at home was left undone.

What kept them there when the two months' duty was over? It may have been a kind of loyalty to an idea of England, or a kind of unanswered questioning that could be called public opinion – or perhaps, filtering down through the ranks, the personal influence of a king who still knew that any moment, any day, the wind might change and the enemy might come. A few more weeks, he must have told them all, and we shall be safe until spring.

Snorri says Harald Hardrada, on the coast of Norway, also waited for a favourable wind. His crews could row, but nobody wants to row if he can sail, and he did not have to wait long. The wind he wanted, of course, was the opposite of the wind that William wanted, a wind from the north-east; and it began in Norway at just about the same moment it began in Normandy. On 12 August, or within a day or two, Harald arrayed his splendid ships off the mountainous island of Solund and led his crews of happy berserkers out to sea. They crossed to the Shetland Islands. That first leg of their voyage is two hundred miles, twice the length of the crossing that William faced, but it was a simple routine affair for a Viking fleet. However, it did illustrate their principal weakness, which was setting and steering a course. Some of the ships missed Shetland altogether and carried on till they sighted the Orkney Islands a hundred miles beyond. Harald stayed a short time in Shetland, which was one of his outlying dominions, and then sailed on to Orkney.

Here there are hints of royal feasting. It was a long time since a reigning King of Norway had visited the earldom of Orkney, longer still since any had done so with a whole fleet, elated in antici-pation of conquest; and never perhaps had a king arrived with his queen and two eligible daughters. As it happened, Earl Torfinn had two eligible sons, whose names were Paul and Erlend. The occasion demanded the greatest celebration the islands could provide.

But the King did not stay long for the banqueting: the season was late for war. Many men of Orkney, infected by the excitement, came in to join his standard. He left the Queen and princesses there, in the care of Torfinn: Paul and Erlend went with him to dis-tinguish themselves beneath his eye. About the end of the month he sailed again, to cross the tide-race of the Pentland Firth and follow the coast of Scotland to the southward: and the wind was still behind him.

In the English Channel there was not a breath of a southerly wind for a month: extraordinary weather that no sailor in those seas, either then or now, would believe could ever happen.* The Normans watched the sky with growing astonishment and self-doubt. They had prayed and were praying for a southerly wind; the end of the summer was dangerously near: it seemed that God might intend to defeat their purpose by denying them their wind.

But on the morning of 12 September the flags and banners at last were blowing in the opposite direction. The Duke gave the order,

---

* Recently, ten years of daily observations in August have averaged one day of calm, eight days of winds between north and east, and twenty days between south and west.

there was a hectic scramble to launch the ships and load the horses, gear and men. At high water the ships were cast off and drifted down the river on the first of the ebb; and the army, hopeful but apprehensive, was committed to the sea.

Within the next twenty-four hours, the very thing happened that everyone had dreaded: the wind veered to the west and began to blow in earnest.

Several historians in the past hundred years have believed that William made this voyage without intending to go to England, but only to move his fleet from the mouth of the Dives to the mouth of the Somme, and thereby to make the final crossing shorter. That is the strangest of misapprehensions, which is disproved at once by the chart of the Channel. The river Dives is in the Bay of the Seine, and to get out of the bay the fleet had to clear its eastern extremity, thirty miles away, which is Cap d'Antifer. The course from the Dives to this headland, in modern terms, is 015° true, which is also precisely the course to Hastings. In other words, when the fleet sailed out of the Dives, and for at least thirty miles beyond, the wind stood fair for England. It is unthinkable that Duke William, after a month of waiting and praying for that very wind, sailed out of the Dives with any intention but to land in England.

Not even William of Poitiers, who firmly believed the Duke could do no wrong, pretended this voyage was anything but a disaster. The fleet, he says, was driven by a west wind towards the harbour of St Valery, which is in the estuary of the Somme. It need not have been a very serious gale. They may not even have known they had gone off course. In clear weather they would have known from the sun or stars, but if they were out of sight of land and the sky was heavily overcast, as it would have been in a westerly wind, the less experienced helmsmen would have steered by the wind and followed it round when it veered. In a beam wind and sea, the fleet could neither go on nor go back to where it had started: heavily laden ships would certainly have taken water and seemed to be in danger of being swamped. The coast runs almost straight from Cap d'Antifer to the west-north-west, and has not a single natural harbour except the inconspicuous mouths of a few small rivers until St Valery fifty miles away. Disorganized by the change of wind far out at sea, scattered perhaps in the dark, with the cargoes of horses and lands-men, each separate helmsman had to run before the wind and sea along that empty coast, searching in growing desperation for an opening in it where there was shelter. Some of them failed: ships were wrecked on the shore or lost at sea; the survivors came into St Valery exhausted, very justifiably frightened, and looking for someone to blame. Many deserted: the storm marked the end of summer, the Norman invasion was on the brink of failure, it started to pour with rain, and the wind went back to the north.

William of Poitiers, in praise of the Duke, reveals how serious his problems had become: 'Daunted neither by the delay, nor the contrary wind, nor the loss of ships, nor even the craven flight of many who broke faith with him, he commended himself with prayers and gifts and vows to the protection of heaven. In his adversity he prudently hid his lack of supplies by increasing the daily rations and, so far as he could, he caused those who had perished in the storm to be secretly buried. By varied exhortations he put courage into the fearful and confidence into those who were cast down. Also he made pious and fervent supplication that the wind which was still adverse might be made favourable to him, and to this end he caused to be brought outside the church the body of St Valery himself, that confessor beloved of God. And all who hoped to set out on the invasion joined him in this act of Christian humility.'

All through the year, there had never been a moment when William could call a halt: he was always compelled to go on. The compulsion now, at this last moment, was stronger than ever. He had always said he would invade that year. If he failed, his reputation would never recover. If he disbanded his army, he could hardly hope to recruit it again in the spring. If he abandoned his ships where they were, not even in Normandy but in the domain of the Count of Ponthieu, he could not expect to find them intact at the end of a winter. If he could not be in England within a few days, he was a beaten man. But if he had known what had happened in the Isle of Wight, he might have found some comfort; for Harold's problems, at just the same moment, had also come to their crisis.

'When it was the Nativity of St Mary,' the Anglo-Saxon Chronicle says, 'the men's provisions were gone, and no man could keep them there any longer. They were allowed to go home.' The Nativity of St Mary was 8 September, four days before Duke William's awful voyage.

One often has to read between the lines of the Chronicle's economical style, and there was obviously more to the trouble in the island than it says: feeding the men was a basic problem that had been growing for weeks, but an army's food does not suddenly come to an end on a certain day. The fyrd has often been blamed for going home too soon, against Harold's wishes. But I am inclined to think the date had been agreed for quite a long time, and that it was probably not the fyrd but the crews of the ships, or their owners, who had proposed the Nativity of St Mary as the day when they could finally say the Normans were not coming.

Everywhere in Europe then, from Norway to the Mediterranean, seafaring was only a summer occupation: nobody put to sea in winter for more than a very short trip. Sailors are men of custom, and there must have been an accepted date in autumn when the lore of the sea said prudent mariners should be at home in harbour, with their ships hauled safely ashore. The date would be earlier in the north than it was in the south: in England it would certainly not be later than the equinox, which is a notorious time for the first of the winter gales. The equinox is 22–23 September but in 1066, since the Julian calendar had lagged six days behind the seasons, it was 16 September. But people normally thought in terms of the church calendar, and much the most probable customary date for the laying up of ships would be the beginning of Ember Week, which marks the transition from summer to winter in the church's year. That was 14 September.

By then, one may suppose, the sailors in the island expected to be home, and they needed a few days to get there. The Nativity of

St Mary, six days before, was a very reasonable date to break camp and begin to pack up for the journey. The same thing has happened, at just the same time of year, whenever the English have been threatened with invasion – by Phillip of Spain, Napoleon and Hitler. They have patiently watched the coast all summer, and in the middle of September – using the modern calendar – have sighed with relief and relaxed, confident that the invasion season is over and winter weather at sea will look after England's defence.

At all events, it had been a remarkable achievement by Harold to have raised an army and navy bigger than any king before him, and much more remarkable still to have kept it intact for over three months with nothing to do. And if this explanation is somewhere near the trend of the weeks of discussion, the fyrd are not to be blamed for going home: they had loyally stayed six weeks beyond their feudal duty. Nor can the sailors really be blamed for saying no reasonable seaman would try to bring a whole fleet across the Channel any later in the year. Probably Harold agreed with them, and willingly let them go. Of course they were all wrong: for Duke William was not behaving as a reasonable seaman.

So the fleet left. The chartered ships made for the Cinque Ports or whatever other harbours they had come from. Harold's own ships sailed round to the Thames and up the river to London. Some delayed a day or two, and that was too long. 'Many perished before they came home,' the Chronicle says: it must have been the same storm that broke up William's fleet – and if William's fleet had come a little farther, the scattered ships of both fleets would have met off the English coast, each fighting against the storm and quite unable to fight against the enemy. The fyrd went home. Harold left Bosham between 13 and 16 September: he never went home again. He rode with the house-carls to London, a two days' march through the Sussex forest, across the North Downs and finally over London Bridge to a welcome in the city. Perhaps he rode with a nagging doubt still lurking in his mind, or perhaps with contentment that the danger was past and he had a winter to make sure of his defences.

In London he went to bed with a crippling pain in his leg: and in London, either two or three days later, the message came that Harald Hardrada had landed two hundred and thirty miles away in Northumbria and burned the town of Scarborough to the ground.

York

September 20-25

The gale on 13 September was the start of a period of a month and
a day packed with coincidences that are hardly credible and yet are
certainly true. Here were two rulers with their fleets and armies,
William and Harald Hardrada, each bent on the conquest of
England, some three hundred miles apart, acting quite independently,
and neither, so far as anyone can tell, suspecting for a moment that
the other was there: and between them Harold, who knew about
William but did not know where he was, and who only heard of
Harald Hardrada's menace when a week was already past. Time
and again in these thirty-two frantic days, one can see that if one
event had chanced to happen one day later or one day earlier than
it did – if anyone had hurried even more or paused a little longer –
all the later events would have happened differently, and nothing
whatever in the history of England since would have been the same.

When Harold heard of Harald Hardrada's landing he did not pause
at all, but instantly ordered the house-carls to be ready to march.
Miracles come into the story now and then, and remind one that its

people had a direct uncomplicated faith: the *Vita Haroldi Regis*, written by a humble monk of Waltham Abbey in 1216, records that Harold spent a sleepless night, kept awake by the pain in his leg and the dread that he felt too sick to lead the long march to North- umbria. In the same night, King Edward appeared to an abbot named Elfin, told him the troubled thoughts of the King and sent him with a message: in heaven the holy King had interceded with God, who had granted Harold victory and the relief of his pain. 'So King Harold, to speak briefly, is cured by divine favour and en- couraged by heavenly words.' One can say a pain is psychosomatic and a cure is made by suggestion, but it does not make much difference. The same morning, Harold led the house-carls through the city, two or three thousand tough professional soldiers, self- disciplined and self-assured, clattering through the streets on their shaggy ponies with their coats of mail across the saddle-bows and their spears and axes by their sides, out by the Bishopsgate and up the deserted Roman road towards the north.

The burning of Scarborough was exactly the sort of thing that Harald Hardrada had always done, in Sicily, North Africa and Denmark. It was an unimportant place, not much more than a fishing village, but it has a steep hill on a promontory and no doubt it caught his eye as he came down the coast. He burned it by one of his tricks. His men built a very large bonfire on top of the hill, and when it was burning merrily they threw and pushed it all down on the roofs of the houses below. There was really not much point in it, except that it was fun.

He had met Tostig again somewhere farther north and they were going together to York, the capital city of Tostig's old earldom and the most important place in the north of England.

York is twenty-five miles inland from Scarborough, but it can be approached from the south by rivers, the Humber and then the Ouse, something like ninety miles of inland water. Harald knew as well as anyone that the sailing season was over, and he needed a winter harbour for his ships. So he chose to go to York by river. They sailed into the Humber and rowed up the narrow winding

Ouse, and no doubt used a rising tide to help them and to float them off if they ran aground. They stopped near a village called Riccall, some nine miles south of the city.

To take a large seagoing fleet so far inland, and in a hostile country, was something nobody but a Viking would have thought of. If there were anything like the number of ships that Snorri said, they would have occupied miles of river; and if any Englishman was lurking in the low-lying marshy meadows and watched them coming – the dragons' heads projecting above the river banks – he must have been a very frightened man. Harald may have hoped to row into York and terrify the people there, but there was every reason to stop when they came to Riccall. For one thing, the river was only just wide enough there for the bigger ships to turn round. For another, a large tributary, the Wharfe, joins the Ouse two miles above the village, and above the junction the river is even smaller and the tide is weaker. And finally, a small English fleet had retreated before the Norsemen as they came, and vanished up the Wharfe. Harald would have despised it; but still, if he had gone up the Ouse the English might have come out of the Wharfe again, and it was better to have them up the river than down it. Even a small fleet, if it had determined crews, could have blocked the river below him and shut him in.

On Tuesday, 19 September, the same day that the news of Scarborough reached London, the ships were all in place, moored fore and aft to stop them swinging with the tide and sticking across the river in the mud. Early next morning, as Harold marched out of London, the Viking army scrambled ashore with its battle gear and cheerfully marched up the river bank to York.

Both the northern earls were in the city, Edwin of Mercia and Morkere of Northumbria, the man the earldom had chosen in place of Tostig. They were both very young – Edwin the elder brother may have been eighteen by then – and they may have been very dependent on each other, because they almost always appear together in history. Nor do they often appear as heroic figures. But since Scarborough they had collected all the men they could, and they marched out of York together to challenge Harald Hardrada.

Neither of them had ever fought a major battle before, nor had their armies, and Harald had been fighting battles since long before they were born. The two armies met head-on at Fulford, which is just over a mile outside the city gates.

Fulford is now a suburb of York, and not very much can be seen of its battlefield. Then, it was a featureless bit of land, a quarter or a third of a mile across, between the river on the west side and a dyke on the east, which bordered a deep and watery marsh. And there are only very meagre accounts of what happened on 20 September: stories of battles are usually told by the winners, and the winners at Fulford were losers a few days later. Snorri gives much the fullest account of Harald Hardrada's campaign, but even he makes Fulford seem a short, elementary and very bloody fight. Both armies drew up some kind of line to face the other, strongest and thickest near the river bank. The English were first to attack, on the other flank by the marsh where Morkere was in command, and they beat the Norsemen back. Harald Hardrada saw his men running and thought for a moment he would be surrounded: he had a blast blown on the horn and unfurled his battle standard – it was called Landeyda, Land-Ravager, a white standard with a black raven on it – and his army counter-attacked with their berserk fury. In the slaughter the English broke and ran, some up the river and some down, and so many were driven into the marsh that the Norsemen's poet sang in triumph:

> 'Waltheof's fighters, bitten with weapons,
> There lay dead, deep in the marshes,
> So that the war-keen Norsemen
> Could cross on corpses only.'*

This grim and improbable image, of rivers or marshes choked with bodies and the victors walking over them, is not an uncommon boast in early battle stories. But although the Battle of Fulford may not have lasted an hour, the victory was thorough.

Harald Hardrada and Tostig entered the city with a bodyguard but left the army outside: they wanted the place as a capital, not a

---

* The Norsemen believed that Waltheof Earl of Huntingdon was there, but they were wrong.

ruin. The city surrendered; bewildered, with their army gone, there was nothing else the people of York could do. Many had fled, but no account mentions the earls, whether they had gone or whether they met Tostig face to face. Harald demanded hostages, which was his right, and there is an unattractive glimpse of Tostig in Snorri's story: 'the sons of the foremost men were taken, according to Tostig's knowledge of all the men in the town.' In his old capital, not a single friend came out to greet him. That evening, the invaders left the city again, crossed the field of battle among the corpses, and all went back rejoicing to the ships at Riccall: and Tostig went with them.

There is a curious air of leisure and festivity over the next four days. Harald behaved as if he thought he had had an easy victory and the whole campaign was over – as if, after Denmark had resisted him for fifteen years, most of England had fallen in a single day. Indeed he had reason to think the defeat of both the earls and the fall of York had given him the north of England, and that Tostig's promise would be fulfilled and friends would soon come flocking in to join him, and that he could challenge Harold from a secure position of strength or perhaps, like Knut and Edmund, agree to divide the kingdom. The Anglo-Saxon Chronicle says the men of York 'agreed to full peace, so that they should all go with him south and this land subdue.' But he stayed in his ships and made no effort to go to the city again: either because he did not trust its promises, or because he did not trust his army near such a tempting prize. Meantime he demanded more hostages, five hundred in all, not only from the city but from all the surrounding shire. The English promised to find five hundred acceptable men and bring them to surrender to him on Monday 25.

The place agreed for the surrender was the village of Stamford Bridge. That is stated by the Chronicle, but Snorri's story, at this particular point, dissolves into total confusion, and nobody has ever explained why Stamford Bridge was chosen, why the hostages could not surrender at Riccall, or why Harald's army could not fetch them from the gates of the city. Perhaps it was simply as good a place as any, and easily found by both sides – seven miles east of

York, where the road to the coast crosses over the river Derwent, another tributary of the Ouse. As the crow flies it was thirteen miles from Riccall, and no doubt a good bit more by whatever tracks there were.

'On Monday,' Snorri says, regaining his eye for detail, 'when Harald had had his breakfast, he had the landing signal blown.' He divided his army, two-thirds to come with him to Stamford Bridge and one-third to look after the ships. Tostig came with him: Olav the King's son and Paul and Erland of Orkney stayed with the ships. It was a fine morning and the sun was warm, and the King was so sure the fighting was over that they all left their coats of mail on board the ships and set off for a comfortable walk in their shirts or tunics, carrying helmets and shields and of course their spears and axes or swords. Some had bows and arrows, and they were all very merry.

At Stamford Bridge they saw not a rabble of hostages but an army coming towards them on the road from York. Harald Hard-rada called for Tostig and asked him what army it could be. Tostig said he thought it might mean trouble – but it might be his friends and kinsmen coming to ask for mercy and make their vows to the King. It was the final forlorn expression of his delusion. Snorri says 'the army grew greater the nearer it came, and it looked like a sheet of ice when the weapons glittered.'

It was Harold of England: and his march was one of the signal feats of military history. One cannot be perfectly certain of all the dates, but the best of evidence is that he marched out of London on the morning of Wednesday, 20 September and was in the village of Tadcaster, a hundred and ninety miles from London and ten from York, on the morning of Sunday 24. At Tadcaster his road crossed the river Wharfe, and he halted to talk to the crews of the ships that had taken refuge there. Perhaps on the road he had met some messengers coming south, but at Tadcaster he had the first certain news of the enemy fleet at Riccall, the Battle of Fulford and the surrender of York. He rode straight on to the city, where the people welcomed him as a saviour. That night he posted men at the gates and on the roads, so that Harald Hardrada should not discover he was there, and at dawn he marched out again for the meeting at Stamford Bridge. And not only that. At the end of the march his army was much bigger than when he started: at all the villages up the Roman road he had rallied the fyrd to join him, and outriders must have combed the country on either side with the shouted news that he needed every man. Finally, in that night at York, he entirely revived the townsmen's shattered morale, so that they followed him out in the morning not to confirm their surrender but to fight again.

It was no mean feat of horsemanship and stamina: the Chronicle says he rode by night and day. It was marvellous as a feat of leadership – to infect a whole army with the same driving sense of urgency, to have the strength at the end of the march to inspire the men of York, and then to bring them all into battle without a pause. Here is proof, if proof is demanded, that Harold possessed the sympathy and loyalty of the English. Nobody knows how the march was organized: from the speed of it, one would judge it was scarcely organized at all – that no soldier waited to be told what to do or to have things done for him, but that each of them expected to carry his own provisions, look after himself and his pony, stop when the leader stopped and go on again whenever the horn was blown. And here is one of the sets of coincidences: if Harold had still been in Bosham when the first message arrived, or if his army had lagged a half-day on the march, or if Harald Hardrada had spent three days instead of four in his negotiations – then the Norsemen would have had their five hundred hostages when Harold arrived, and he would have had to treat with Harald Hardrada instead of fighting him: which was what he marched out to do soon after dawn on Monday morning.

Stamford Bridge is still a village on the river crossing, and the terrain of it can easily be identified with accounts of the battle that was fought that sunny September day. The river Derwent is not very big, but too big to cross by anything but a bridge, and it had one in Saxon times. There is an eighteenth-century water mill now between

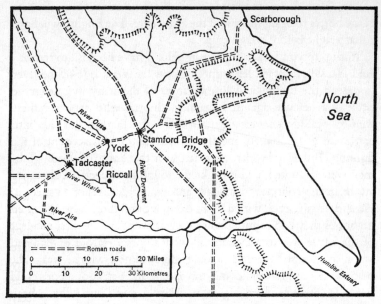

Stamford Bridge

the village green and the river: its machinery still goes round, but the whole thing has been converted to a bar and restaurant, with a discothèque in the grain-loft on Saturdays. The Saxon bridge was a little way above the weir of this incongruous mill, two or three hundred yards upstream from the present bridge. When Harald Hardrada sighted the glittering army, a mile or so away at the top of the gentle hill towards York, his own troops were scattered, leisurely and unsuspecting, around both ends of the bridge, some on the York side of the river, in flat water-meadows which are a caravan site now, and some on the rising ground of the other bank.

'There is certainly trouble,' he said to Tostig as the army approached. 'This must be the King himself. What do you propose to do?'

'We must retreat to the ships,' Tostig said, 'and collect the rest of the men and the armour and fight them there – or board the ships so that their horsemen cannot attack us.'

'No,' Harald Hardrada said, 'we will send three men on the best of the horses to bring the rest of the army here. The English will have a sharp fight before we give up.'

'It is up to you to decide,' Tostig said. 'I have no wish to retreat.' And Harald Hardrada left some men on the York side of the river to defend the bridge, and formed most of the army in a defensive circle – a defence against horsemen. Snorri, who reported these weirdly realistic conversations, believed the English did ride into battle: he was mistaken, and the mistake distorts his account of the fighting. But Harald Hardrada had seen that most of the Englishmen were mounted, and it is likely enough he expected a mounted attack in the continental manner and made his defence to meet it. He and Tostig, each with a small troop around him, were mounted on horses they had captured since they arrived; and the first incident of the battle was that Harald fell off his horse. Harold of England was near enough to see, and asked if anyone knew who he was – 'the man with the blue tunic and the special helmet.' Somebody told him. 'He is certainly a big man,' Harold said, 'but I think he is going to be unlucky.'

Then Harold rode out in front of his army with a score of men, so close to the Norsemen that he could talk to them. 'Is Earl Tostig in your army?' he shouted across the gap.

'That is no secret,' somebody answered. 'You can find him here.' Tostig came forward and the brothers confronted each other.

'Your brother sends you greetings,' Harold said, hiding his identity from the Norsemen. 'He offers you peace and all Northumbria. Rather than have you refuse and insist on battle, he would give you a third of the kingdom.'

Tostig answered: 'That is different from the trouble and shame of last winter. If I had had this offer then, many a man who is dead now would have been alive, and England would have been a better place.' And indeed it was a complete reversal of Harold's earlier acts; one can only suppose that Edwin and Morkere, the two young northern earls, had so disgraced themselves in his eyes by surrendering that he was willing to depose them – and that after the night's discussions in York he knew that the people were ashamed and would agree.

'If I accept,' Tostig shouted, 'what will my brother offer King Harald Hardrada for his work?'

'He said something about that too,' Harold said. 'Something about six feet of English earth – or a bit more as he is such a big man.'

'Then go and tell King Harold to be ready for battle,' Tostig said. 'I can never have it said among the Norsemen that Earl Tostig deserted their King in face of a fight. We shall stick together: die with honour, or win England by victory.'

Harold rode back to his army. Harald Hardrada had been watching and listening, but had not understood the English conversation. He asked Tostig, 'Who was that man? He spoke well.'

'That was King Harold,' Tostig said.

'Why did you not tell me?' Harald Hardrada said. 'He came so near he would never have escaped.'

'I know,' Tostig said. 'He was taking risks for such a chief, and you could have caught him. He offered me peace and power. I might have been his killer if I had said who he was. But I would rather he was my killer.'

'Quite a small man,' Harold Hardrada said, 'but he stood well in his stirrups.' And he made up a verse:

'Forth we go in our lines
Without our armour, against the blue blades.
The helmets glitter: I have no armour.
Our shrouds are down in those ships.'

Battle began: a hand-to-hand battle in the old Viking style, fought on foot with swords and spears and battle-axes. It began on the York side of the river in the water meadows, and the Norsemen were beaten back across the bridge and into the river itself; and here again, this time in the English accounts, one has the proverbial image of a river so choked with bodies that the victors could walk over it, a feat even more inconceivable in the Derwent than in the marshes of Fulford. Here also, a story which had all the makings of legend and is still the best-remembered thing about the battle: that one enormous Viking stood on the bridge and defended it single-handed. That story has a curious origin: it first appears in one, but only one, of the versions of the Anglo-Saxon Chronicle, and strangely enough the version written in the faraway abbey of Abingdon; and it has been added to the end of the manuscript in a different and less literate hand, as if a visiting monk from the north had insisted the story ought to be recorded. Several writers in the next century took it up and added to it: one of them says the solitary Viking, who must have been a true berserker, killed forty Englishmen. And all of them agree that nobody could move him until one man found a boat, or a swill-tub, and drifted down the river in it unseen, under the bridge, and speared him up through the chinks in the wooden deck.*

When that hero was dead, the English army charged across the bridge and the battle began again on the other side. There is no description in detail of the later part of it: and what factual description could there be of thousands of men all fighting hand-to-hand, each intent only on enemies within the seven-foot swing of an axe? The English broke the Norsemen's line; and seeing it break, Harald Hardrada himself went berserk and charged out flailing about him two-handed: 'neither helmet nor mail could stand against him.' Among innumerable enemies, there was only one end for a berserker: the old warrior, the veteran of a lifetime of battles, fell dead, hit in the throat by an arrow – perhaps an expert huntsman in Harold's army, trained to shoot running deer.

The battle stopped. Tostig took up the Land-Ravager, Hardrada's fallen standard. In the pause while everyone got his breath, Harold offered peace to Tostig and the remaining Norsemen, but their blood was up and they shouted their war-cries and began again. The men from Riccall arrived. They had run in their chain-mail. Some were so exhausted they were almost unfit to fight, some even collapsed and died without a wound; but some infected by the battle-madness threw off their mail and waded into the bloodshed. Towards the evening, at some moment and by some ghastly blow that was unrecorded, Tostig died; and as darkness fell the survivors

---

* A local historian in the nineteenth century said the people of Stamford Bridge still held an annual feast in commemoration, when they ate pies that were shaped like swill-tubs; but they seem to have forgotten the custom now.

fled for Riccall and the ships.

In terms of sheer slaughter this was the greatest battle that had ever been fought in England; lasting from morning to dusk, it was the longest. Seventy years later, the place was still marked by heaps of bones. It was also the most complete of victories: an untold number of Englishmen were killed, but the Norsemen's army, refusing to surrender, was destroyed.

But Harold, who had twice tried to stop it, seems never to have been a man to glory in slaughter, or even in victory. The next day, King Harald Hardrada's son Olav came to give himself up, with Paul and Erlend the two young earls of Orkney, who had all escaped because they were left at Riccall. Harold wearily asked them to promise never to come to England again, and told them they could take what ships they needed and go home, with all their survivors – a forgiveness in victory rare in any era. They rowed down the Ouse again and out of the Humber, and now with a southerly wind they sailed back towards Orkney to break the news to the Queen and the two princesses there, and then to Norway. There were so few of them left that they took only twenty-four of the ships of Harald Hardrada's fleet.

While the Norsemen retreated, Harold's army rested, and he worked to restore some order into the organization of York, where the defeat of Fulford and the sudden surrender had produced a crop of recriminations among the leading citizens. He did not depose the earls: he spent some days in diplomacy, soothing outraged feelings as he so often had before he was King. He also had an argument with his army, who said he had not shared out the trophies of battle fairly: perhaps he had insisted on keeping the Viking fleet, which would have been a tremendous national asset.

About a week after the battle, when the Norsemen were safely gone, everyone was calm and contented enough for a victory feast to be held, and it is said it was during the feast that the message came from the south: Duke William had landed at Pevensey.

The English Channel

September 28

If God intervenes in such things, as everyone then believed, Duke William's prayers had been answered more wisely than he knew: the southerly wind he had prayed for had been withheld for six weeks, and was granted on the very day after the Battle of Stamford Bridge, when Harold's army was counting its dead and nursing its wounds and was two hundred and fifty miles away from the coast it had guarded all summer. Stamford Bridge was on the 25, the south wind started at St Valery on the night of the 26, William sailed on the 27 and landed on the 28; and he did not know how lucky or how blessed he had been.

For this part of the story, the Normans' sea-crossing, their landing and the subsequent battle, the principal sources are the *Carmen de Hastingae Proelio*, the Song of the Battle of Hastings, ascribed to Guy, Bishop of Amiens, and the *Gesta Guillielmi*, the Deeds of William, written by the chaplain William of Poitiers; and they are augmented by the Bayeux tapestry. All the later writers made use of these accounts, especially the chaplain's – though some of them, as usual, added stories of their own. There is practically no account of these events from the English side; for many years after, the English were too devastated by their disaster to write any more than the curt entries in the Anglo-Saxon Chronicle.

The *Carmen* is a history in over eight hundred lines of Latin verse which was probably written within six months of the battle. It seems to have been an unpopular work in its time, because the bishop was a Frenchman not a Norman and tended to praise the French contingents in William's army at the expense of the Normans. Sometimes he was less than polite about William himself. The chaplain began to write his account, in Latin prose, about five years later; and he, on the other hand, praised the Normans at the expense of their allies and especially made William a superhuman hero. The tapestry, a few years after that, is supposed to have been commissioned by William's half-brother Bishop Odo to decorate his new cathedral at Bayeux, and it gives Odo and some of his servants more prominence than they deserved.

So while all these accounts are naturally prejudiced against the English, each of them also has its own private prejudice. The *Carmen* is the most level-headed of the three. But it was lost within twenty or thirty years of being written, and was only discovered again in 1826, when a very early manuscript of it was found in the Royal Library in Brussels. Consequently, the Anglo-Norman writers of the twelfth century mainly based their accounts on that of the chaplain William of Poitiers. His account remained the dominant source for seven hundred and fifty years. Since the *Carmen* was rediscovered, scholars have used it to balance the chaplain's prejudice, which was outrageous, but he still remains the basis of what one might call the school-book histories.

The chaplain evidently used the *Carmen* himself as one of his sources, but he altered it to the greater glory of his hero. His whole thesis was that Duke William was a man who never sinned, never fought unjustly and never suffered any human weakness. His praise is often so absurdly obsequious that its effect on a modern reader is the opposite of what he intended – it makes the Duke himself seem a clown, which is certainly one thing he was not. But still, it is not very difficult to separate the praise and propaganda from the rest, and to compare the residual facts with those of the *Carmen*. Neither of these writers seems to have crossed the Channel with William, but both of them knew many men who did. Writing when the events were fresh in memory, they both had plenty of critics to correct them in matters of fact – among them the Duke himself. Nobody could correct the chaplain's servile attitude, and if the story has ludicrous moments it is mostly the fault of this humourless clergyman.

In the Normans' belief, what had changed the wind at last was the parading of the relics of St Valery and their own offerings: after the shrine was brought out of the church, they threw so many coins onto it that the carpet it stood on was hidden. When, in the early morning of 27 September, the weathervane on the church tower was seen to be pointing south, there was a wild scramble to get away before it changed again: 'some were calling for their knights or their companions but most, forgetful alike of followers, companions or provisions, were only eager not to be left behind.' It says a lot for the army's faith in God and the Duke that enough of them were willing to try again after their horrid experience of the sea a fortnight before – and to try it so unbelievably late in the year. The Duke urged them on board, but when they were ready and the tide was right it was afternoon. He sent a herald round to tell them to wait in the mouth of the harbour until they saw a light at his masthead in the night, and then to make sail and follow it. From the mouth of the Somme with a reasonable wind it is only a twelve-hour crossing to the coast of England. By that time in the year the nights are getting long, and they did not want to approach the coast in the dark.

He waited offshore in his own ship, which was called the *Mora*. Nobody knows what the name meant, but the ship was the contribution of his wife Matilda, and the most attractive suggestion is that Mora was her family nickname: in most languages it has a motherly sound. With him on board, one may suppose, were a crew of twenty-four oarsmen, his own servants, squires and pages, a few of his close companions, possibly Bishop Odo, Robert of Mortain and

William FitzOsbern – and finally, the best of the helmsmen Normandy could provide, and some pilots, probably Flemings, who had sailed the coast of England and knew it by sight. Some time in the night, he gave the pilots their orders, the masthead lantern was lit, the watchmen saw it through the darkened fleet, and all the sails were hoisted.

One has to pause at this moment to work out what orders he could possibly have given. The name of Hastings is so embedded in English history that one tends to think William had chosen to land there as part of a detailed military plan. Yet on second thoughts, could he have known enough about the topography of England to have made any closely reasoned choice? And if he had chosen a place, what chance did he have of reaching it from the sea? And finally, if he had chosen Hastings, why did he first land at Pevensey, ten miles beyond it?

The invasion had only been thought of within the year. Before that, there was no reason at all for Normans to look at the country-side of England with a careful strategic eye; and after it, though William may have had spies, it is very hard to imagine that any experienced Norman rode all along the coast surveying it from the saddle to find the things an invading army needed – which were a harbour where the ships could shelter, a route inland that a mounted army could march on, a countryside with enough farm stock to feed them, and a base they could defend.

The move to St Valery had narrowed the choice by half. From there, to go any farther west than Beachy Head was simply to make the voyage longer; and one can observe all through the Middle Ages that when knights were obliged to go to sea, their one idea was to get ashore again as quickly as they could. East of the high white cliffs of Beachy Head there are forty-five miles of low-lying land before the cliffs of Dover, only interrupted by the lower sand-stone cliffs near Hastings. So from St Valery, William had to land within that forty-five miles, or at Dover itself, or else beyond Dover on the coast that runs north to Sandwich.

The low-lying coast has changed a lot in the past nine hundred years. At that time, it had five harbours which now have entirely silted up and disappeared. The farthest west was Pevensey; next, smaller but still big enough, was Bulverhythe, close to the little town of Hastings; then a very small harbour at Hastings itself; then Rye, the most extensive of all; and then Romney. East of Romney, Folkestone and Dover had small usable harbours, and round the corner was Sandwich, which was a principal cross-Channel port and a base for the royal ships.

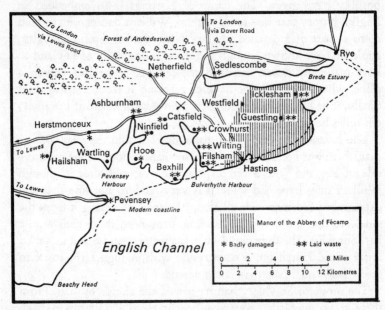

The Sussex coast

There was one extremely significant exception to William's limited knowledge of the coast and the countryside behind it. The evidence of it is in Domesday Book, which was compiled on William's orders in 1086 to record the ownership and taxable value of the landed estates of England. Some years before the invasion, King Edward had given two large estates to the Norman Abbey of Fécamp. One was at Steyning, five miles inland to the west of Brighton, and

146

Harold had revoked this gift and reclaimed the land for the crown. The other was a manor called Rameslie. The name has disappeared entirely, but the estate included the coast from Hastings to Winchelsea and most of the country inland to the river Brede – exactly the stretch of land that William's army occupied. There were certainly monks in Fécamp who knew that bit of England intimately and could have told William all about it. Moreover he did discuss the invasion with the Abbot of Fécamp; he is known to have promised he would restore the estate of Steyning. It seems probable that Hastings was William's favourite choice for a landing, not for any strategic reason at all, but simply because he knew more about it, from the monks' descriptions, than he did about anywhere else.

But if that was his first choice, there was still the question of getting there. The course from St Valery to Bulverhythe, the harbour for Hastings, is north-west. That would have been difficult or impossible if his prayers had brought a south-westerly wind, normally the commonest in the Channel: so he must have been prepared in his mind, ever since he was driven to St Valery, to land farther east, at Rye, or possibly Folkestone or Dover, or even at Sandwich. His luck or his prayers held again: the wind came truly south. But he can only have decided on that very day to try for the Hastings area.

When that decision was made, the landfall was up to the pilots, and he gave them a difficult job. There is no direct evidence of how a twelfth-century pilot found his way across the English Channel: the oldest surviving document, which is a book of sailing directions, is dated three hundred years later, and even then the methods were elementary. There were certain known courses from shore to shore, but not many of them; and all of them except the shortest in the Straits of Dover were between conspicuous landmarks which could be easily recognized from the sea. One of these was Beachy Head. It is most unlikely that even in the fifteenth century anyone knew exactly the course from St Valery to Bulverhythe, neither of which was conspicuous or important, and there was no way of finding out except by trial and error. What a Flemish pilot might have known was the course to Beachy Head – his landfall if ever he was going anywhere west along the coast of England.

Any pilot even now who had to make that crossing without a chart or compass, as William's pilots did, would use the ancient method of the Deliberate Error: he would not steer directly towards his objective but to one side of it, so that when he saw the coast he would know which way to turn. Aiming for Beachy Head he would instinctively steer to the north of the recognized course: south of it, he might miss the headland altogether. Nor-west-and-by-west, in a later seaman's language, would be the word that went round the pilots of William's fleet. With luck, when they had run their distance on that course, they would sight the high cliffs on their port bow: Pevensey would be somewhere ahead, and Bulver-hythe off to starboard. But it is a difficult course to steer by the sun or stars, and nobody then or now would feel ashamed if he found himself five miles wrong at the end of it.

Thus the final choice of the Hastings district can only have been made on the day the fleet set sail; and which of the harbours was sighted first was one of the chances of pilotage.

The pilots of the *Mora*, steering straight out to sea that night with the pole star four points and a bit on the starboard bow when they could see it, had a task that nobody would envy. Their hope and no doubt their spoken prayer was to sight a high white cliff in the morning.

But when the morning dawned, there was nothing in sight at all: no cliff, no glimpse of the shore of England and, worst of all, not one of the hundreds of ships that ought to have been astern. An oarsman sent to the masthead shouted down that he could not see anything except the sky and sea. The chaplain, who was certainly no seaman, reported that the Duke cast anchor, which is not a thing one does out of sight of land. But the sail was lowered and the *Mora* stopped.

The Duke, to allay any fear or apprehension among his shipmates, ordered a large repast for himself with a bumper of spiced wine, and sat down to eat and drink with good spirits, as if he had been in a room in his own house: the splendid and calculated courage of that feast, the chaplain said, was worthy of the highest praise of poets. He did not say whether the pilots had any breakfast, or any appetite: they must have been quaking with the dread that they had made some ghastly error, that all their colleagues in the fleet had gone the right way and they alone were lost with the Duke himself.

It was not quite so bad as that: the error was only in the speed of the fleet. The *Mora*, which no doubt was the best of the ships and had the best of the crews, had outsailed all the rest. After the Duke had eaten all he could eat, the oarsman was sent up the mast again and saw four other masts astern; and later he went up a third time, and reported the masts were like the trees in a forest. 'We leave it to the reader to judge,' the chaplain wrote, 'how the confident hope of the Duke was turned to joy, and how from the depths of his heart he gave thanks to God for his mercy.' One might add that the reader may guess what he said to the pilots.

When the fleet came up, the *Mora* got under way again, and at length the land was sighted. No details are given of that landfall, whether it was clear or misty, or what it was the lookouts saw; but it was more than likely the heights of Beachy Head, which are seen from far to seaward. The *Carmen* says the fleet reached harbour at the third hour of the day, which was nine o'clock. But nobody outside the monasteries bothered to know the exact time of day: they just referred to the nearest of the canonical hours of prayer. The third hour, terce, meant no more, in lay affairs, than the middle of the morning, something vaguely earlier than sext, which is noon. From the chaplain's story, one would think the morning must have been well advanced before they were close inshore.

The delay in the night, and the time of high water, provide a probable reason why they went into Pevensey. High water that day was just before noon. Both Pevensey and Bulverhythe were large sheets of inland water which must have had strong tidal streams in their entrances, and it would have been risky if not impossible to try to sail in against the ebb. No doubt the pilots explained their final problem: they must enter harbour quickly, on the last of the flood, or else spend another night at sea. From anywhere off Beachy Head, the nearest harbour was Pevensey, not Bulverhythe, and to catch the tide they altered course towards it.

The crossing had been slow, but an almost complete success. Only two ships had disappeared. One carried an official soothsayer who had prophesied that England would be won without a fight. 'Not much of a soothsayer,' William said, 'if he could not foretell his own death.' The pilots had done well, but as a feat of seamanship it was nothing compared with Viking voyages. The weather had been an astonishing piece of luck, or an astonishing proof of prayer. Above all, the whole enterprise had been a masterpiece of will-power.

Somebody, as the *Mora* stood in for the shore, spotted first the massive walls of the Roman fortress which stood and still stand at Pevensey, and then the gap in the desolate stony beach which was the entrance of the harbour. There is no suggestion in any account that any of them had ever been to Pevensey before.

Some hundreds of English people saw them coming but nobody tried to stop them: nobody could. Pevensey was quite a considerable place, not a mere village but a market town. A special detachment of the fyrd had been there all summer – among them possibly Ulfer the thane of Horstede, which was only a dozen miles away. But they had gone home like the rest of the fyrd three weeks before, and left the little town to look after itself. Fifty-two burgesses or citizens are recorded in Domesday Book. They made their living as merchants, and by pasturing cattle, charging harbour dues and running the trade of the salt pans in the marshes. When the terrible fleet came sailing in, they all did their best to hide.

The Normans leaped ashore prepared for a fight, but perhaps not a serious fight: in the tapestry, when the horses have been persuaded to jump overboard, the knights gallop eagerly forth with shields and lances wearing their coats of mail – but conspicuously they are not wearing helmets, which all of them wear in the later scenes at Hastings. William could hardly have known that Harold's army had gone, but he would always have known the English could not put up more than a skirmish at the moment of landing, and that the battle would come when their army was brought to the spot. Stepping ashore with confidence, according to the *Roman de Rou*, he slipped and fell forward with both his hands on the ground. There was a cry of horror at the evil omen, but he picked himself up and said with ready wit, 'By God's splendour, I have seized the soil of England in both my hands.' But this is one of the perennial stories of early historians, and nobody need believe it: an identical misfortune, and an identical response, were told by Suetonius, some nine hundred years before, about Caesar landing in Africa, and again by Froissart, three hundred years later, about King Edward landing in Normandy on the way to Crécy.

Finding nobody to fight, the second thought of the army was food, to judge again by the tapestry. There were no organized rations; some men had brought something for the voyage, and others had forgotten even that. Knights produced ropes and lassoed the townsmen's cattle, soldiers captured pigs and sheep, fires were lit and cauldrons hung on poles. The leaders are pictured sitting at a table: Bishop Odo presides in the centre, and he ostentatiously has a fish in front of him while the others are offered chickens skewered on arrows: perhaps this leisurely dinner was on the day after the landing, which was Friday. A fort was built inside the Roman walls. The Normans could put up a wooden fort, on a mound with a ditch round it, within a day or two, and it is thought they not only brought the timber with them but brought it pre-fabricated and ready to fit together. William rode out with William FitzOsbern and twenty-five knights to prospect the surrounding country and its people. Some minor disaster overtook them: the ground was so rough that they had to come back on foot – 'a matter doubtless for laughter,' the chaplain wrote, but one that he managed to convert to praise; for his hero came back carrying over his shoulder not only his own chain-mail but also William FitzOsbern's.

Perhaps that undignified reconnaissance persuaded William that Pevensey was not the kind of place he needed. It certainly had a disadvantage: the only good road out of it was an ancient Roman road, which ran due west to Lewes fifteen miles away before it turned north towards London – the road the Horstede people knew on the other side of their river. There was no other route inland except a marshy track round the harbour. I have suggested he only went into Pevensey because the crossing was slow and the pilots had steered for Beachy Head; and having seen the place, he decided very soon to move to the countryside that belonged to the Abbey of Fécamp.

It was a much more difficult move than it looks on the ground today. What used to be Pevensey Harbour is now called Pevensey Levels, ten square miles of flat farm land intersected by dikes and ditches: it is cut off from the sea by a bank of stones and sand which has no gap in it now. But the sluggish rivers that cross the Levels still have the names they had when they were tidal arms of the sea, Wallers Haven, Hurst Haven, Old Haven and Pevensey Haven itself. Now there is a road behind the stony bank, and Hastings is only ten miles away. But then, it was at least thirty miles by the track round the harbour and then round the harbour of Bulverhythe. The army had to put to sea again, or be ferried across the mouth of the harbour, or march the whole way round. There is evidence that William divided the army: sent some of the ships to carry equipment, ferried the foot-soldiers over the harbour mouth, and let the knights ride round.*

This evidence again is an incidental product of Domesday Book. Listing every village, it often gives their taxable value at three different times: just before the invasion, just after it, and twenty years later when the survey was made. Some places came through the invasion without any change, but many fell in value. Some had a disastrous fall which indicates that they were badly damaged, their stock was seized or their people killed or scattered. Some in the south of Sussex have the grim entry 'wasta'; they were laid waste. From these methodical valuations, one can trace the movements of William's army.

A double trail of destruction leads from Pevensey to Hastings. Pevensey itself lost half its population: the number of burgesses fell from fifty-two to twenty-seven. Round the northern shore of the

---

* This might be thought a minor mistake in the Bayeux tapestry. Where the knights gallop off from the landing the caption reads, 'And here the soldiers hurry to Hastings to seize food.' But the tapestry had to keep the story short.

harbour, where the knights went raging past, Hailsham, Herstmonceux and Hooe all lost three-quarters of their value. Wartling escaped: it was on a promontory in the marshes and off the track. Ashburnham, where the track crossed a river, was laid waste: Ninfield and Catsfield just beyond it were badly damaged.

On the other route along the coast where the foot-soldiers marched, the destruction was more thorough. Four villages lay in their path: Bexhill on the coast and Crowhurst, Wilting and Filsham, all near the shore of the harbour of Bulverhythe. All four were laid waste. Leaving these paths of doom and ruin behind it, the army entered the land of the Abbey of Fécamp on 30 September or 1 October. William made his headquarters at Hastings, which was nominally a town but no bigger than a village, and put up another wooden fort.

He has sometimes been accused of encouraging destruction in order to lure Harold down to Hastings to fight. But I doubt that he encouraged it: it was simply the natural course of events. The army took the villagers' food because they had not brought any with them; they had to live off the land. Knights had always ravaged villages in hostile countryside, and as for the mercenaries, that was the sort of thing they had come for. It had been remarkable that William prevented plundering when the army was waiting in Normandy: if he had tried to stop it in England, they would have thought he was crazy. Nor can I think that Harold was much influenced by the loss of a score of villages, though one Norman chronicler said he was angry. It was a hazard of war, and even an English army marching through England did no good at all to the villages it passed through.

It is very difficult now to weigh up the tactical merits of a place through the eyes of an army commander so long ago: there are too many unanswerable questions about the ways an army fed and sheltered itself and its horses, and especially how it moved: which roads, for example, in England in October, could stand up to the sudden passage of thousands of horses and men on foot without breaking up into such a bog that the rearguard would be stuck in it?

And there is always the fundamental difference in the point of view. Now, one instinctively thinks of a stretch of country as a map, viewed from above. But then, not even a man of William's status would have thought in terms of maps: he would have viewed the country in his mind's eye as he would have seen it, from eye level.

Yet look at it how one may, Hastings seems to have no advantages, and one cannot think William knowingly chose it for any military reason, or for any better reason than that it was Norman property and the monks had told him what it looked like. It was an isolated little corner of England, a triangle roughly ten miles by six. The river Brede cut right across the north of it in a wide marshy valley, and it was tidal then all the way up to Sedlescombe: the harbour of Bulverhythe shut it off in the west. Even now, both these valleys are obstacles, each with only a single road across it. Then, they were both impassable, and the distance between the ends of their tidal waters was only about four miles. That gap, or isthmus, was hilly and full of steep little valleys, very bad cavalry country. There were pack-horse tracks from village to village, and a track round the head of Bulverhythe harbour, the way the foot-soldiers came in. Apart from that, there was only one road out. A Roman road ran north through the forest to Maidstone, where it joined the road from Dover to London. It crossed the valley of the Brede at Sedlescombe, probably by a tidal ford. But that river crossing seems to have fallen out of use by 1066. Instead, there was a by-pass which, like most of the major Anglo-Saxon tracks, followed the watershed between the two river systems. Another track led off the by-pass to Lewes in the west, with a branch through the forest that joined the Lewes to London road a few miles north of Horstede. By either route, the Dover road or the Lewes road, it was just over sixty miles to London. But to get out of the Hastings triangle an army had to use the track on the watershed.

To be surrounded by water might be an advantage in defence: where there was only one way out, there was only one way in. But that triangle could not be defended long. The army was about five times the normal population. In a fortnight, the Fécamp estate had already been ravaged for food: the monks paid dearly for any advice they had given. Every village was 'wasta', waste, with two exceptions: Hastings itself, where William was, and Westfield which unaccountably escaped. The army could not have wintered where it was. Come what might, William had to move, or starve.

For a week, no word came in from the rest of England. The army was isolated, encamped among the smouldering villages in the little triangle it had won, and the forests beyond lay silent.

The Challenge

October 3-13

In fact, beyond those empty forests, events were moving with a speed that seems astonishing now. The *Roman de Rou* has a story of a thane of Pevensey who hid behind a hill and watched the landing and even the building of the fort, and then escaped and rode all the way to York to tell the King. But this must be one of the poem's romantic decorations. There were several men in Pevensey with official posts that obliged them to do something positive, and their very first reaction – deserted now by the fyrd – would certainly have been to rush off and shout for help. Somebody must have mounted and galloped to Lewes as soon as they saw that the fleet in the offing was foreign; it might have been seen far out at sea from Beachy Head. Before the whole fleet was in harbour, the warning could easily have been in Lewes, and riders well on the way to London before the landing was finished. And soon, behind these urgent messengers, a wave of shock and rumour must have spread by the village tracks, first as warnings from thanes to their neighbours and then reinforced by refugees from the ravaged villages, hoping for food and shelter from the autumn nights.

On either the third or fourth day after the landing, the news reached Harold in York, two hundred and fifty miles away: perhaps he left a relay of riders behind him on the road or even a line of beacons. Four days after that, on 5 October, he had repeated his epic march and was back with the army in London.

It can only have been a weary army, encouraged perhaps by the victory at Stamford Bridge, but smaller by the numbers of dead and wounded it had left behind. Harold himself can hardly have come through that fortnight in the north unscarred in mind or anything but exhausted in his body: eight days of urgent riding, one of battle, five of difficult diplomacy, the double shock – first of the news of the Norse invasion and then of beating that enemy only to find another behind his back – and over it all the loneliness of a king. He did not ride into London with the army, but turned off the road a few miles short of the city and went to the abbey he had built at Waltham.

While Bosham was his family home, Waltham was a spiritual home for Harold. He had built and endowed it and installed its twelve canons during his years as Subregulus, especially to enshrine the Holy Rood. That was a stone figure of Christ on the cross, encased in silver; it had been dug up on top of a hill and nobody knew who had buried it, and among its miracles it had cured Harold of some kind of paralysis when he was a boy. At Waltham he could be sure of a little time to pray in quiet.

Here another miraculous event was recorded. Harold spent the day in prayer, and when he was going out of the church he bowed to the crucifix; and the canons, 'gladdened and terrified', saw the stone image bow its head in reply. It remained with bowed head ever after: the stone appeared to be bent, and the silver neither cracked nor wrinkled. It was taken as an auspicious and wonderful sign, but after the events of the next few days it had to be reinterpreted: a sign that God was to 'take away a shadowy kingdom from this man for whom he preserved a true and everlasting one, that the former might not even be a slight hindrance to his passing to the latter.'

*

On that day when Harold went to Waltham, or a day on either side of it, the first message from the outside world reached William in his camp at Hastings: a man who may have been a Norman rode out of the forest and down the track along the watershed and was accosted by an outpost of the army. But the message he brought was not from Harold, it was from Robert FitzWimark, the Norman who had been present at King Edward's death. Robert, on his mother's side, claimed kinship with William, and was one of the very few men in England whom William might have expected to be a friend. But the message was not friendly. It brought the news that Harold had won a tremendous victory over the Norsemen, and the warning that he was coming with an innumerable army well equipped for war: against them, it said, William's army was no more use than a pack of curs. Robert's advice was that William should be cautious and stay within his defences, or he would run into peril from which he would not escape. William sent a reply: he thanked Robert for his advice and regretted that he had expressed it in an insulting manner. He had no intention of taking it; he proposed to give battle to Harold as soon as possible: and it was then that he claimed he had sixty thousand men and said he would have been eager to fight if he had had only ten thousand.

Two or three days later, a second rider came out of the woods: this time a monk, who brought a message from Harold.

The messages that Harold and William now exchanged are important in understanding the battle they fought. The accounts of them, of course, are Norman or French, and they are all somewhat different. The chaplain says envoys carried the messages from London to Hastings and back: in the *Carmen* and other versions, some are exchanged across the battlefield itself. The contents of the messages also differ, but not very much; clearly they are different interpretations of the same thing.

The chaplain's story is the most circumstantial, and fits in best with Harold's movements. He says that when Harold's monk was brought into William's camp, William, playing for time, pretended to be his own steward and told the man he must say what the message was before he would admit him to his master. Having heard it, he promised the monk an audience on the following day, and spent the evening with his friends composing an answer. Next day, he summoned the monk to a council and made him repeat what he had said.

The message was oral, probably composed in English and delivered in French, but the chaplain gives it verbatim in Latin; so one need not be bound by literal translation. In essence, Harold said William had come to the country unasked, with intentions he did not know. 'He recalls that King Edward first appointed you as his heir, and he remembers he was himself sent to Normandy to assure you of the succession. But he also knows that the same King, his Lord, bestowed on him the kingdom of England when he was dying. Ever since the time when the blessed Augustine came to these shores, it has been the unbroken custom of the English to treat a deathbed request as inviolable. With justice, therefore, he bids you go back to your country with your followers. Otherwise he will break the pact of friendship he made with you in Normandy. And he leaves the choice entirely to you.'

Obviously, if Harold had restated his claim, this is not exactly how he would have done it. Yet it is remarkable that the chaplain gave him a reasonable ground for the claim.

The chaplain then gives William's reply, which his envoy took to Harold. It repeats the same claims that William had always made, Edward's promise and Harold's oath, but omits the claim of hereditary right, which indeed was plausible in Europe but worthless in England. There is one new statement: that Godwin, Archbishop Stigand and two other earls had sworn in Edward's presence to support his choice of William. And it ends: 'I am ready to submit my case against Harold's for judgement either by the law of Normandy or the law of England, whichever he chooses.' If Harold refused, he proposed the quarrel should be settled by single combat between them.

'We have been careful,' the chaplain adds in his naïve but odious style, 'to record this speech in the Duke's own words, for we wish posterity to judge him with favour. Anyone may easily judge that he showed himself wise and just, pious and brave. His argument was so strong that it could not be shaken by Tully himself, the glory of Roman eloquence; and it brought to nought the claims of Harold.' Perhaps his earlier readers agreed. But now, on the contrary, the messages – as he reported them – only seem to confirm once again what was undoubtedly the truth: that both men equally believed their claim was just, one founding his belief on English and the other on Norman customs of inheritance.

William's final offers, if he really made them, had very little meaning; and here again, as so often before, one cannot tell whether words put into his mouth were his own, or were invented by his historians to make 'posterity . . . judge him with favour'. The succession of England could not be decided by Norman law, and had already been decided by English law. If a legal decision went against him, was he really prepared to persuade his army to go peacefully home, without any of the vast rewards he had promised it? As for the offer of single combat, he knew and everyone knew that nobody on the losing side would feel they were bound by the result: whatever way kingdoms had been awarded, it was not that way.

The contents of the messages may be a literary exercise, rather than a word-for-word report, but the chaplain next describes a scene of great significance. The two monks, Harold's and William's envoys, rode back to London together: William's, as one might expect, was a monk of Fécamp who spoke English – he is named in the *Roman de Rou* as Hugh Margot, and no doubt he had lived on the abbey's estate at Hastings. He delivered William's message. 'When Harold heard it,' the chaplain wrote, 'he grew pale and for a long time remained as if he were dumb. And when the monk asked more than once for an answer, he first said, "We march at once," and then added "We march to battle." The monk begged him to reconsider his answer, for the Duke had demanded a single combat, not a battle. Then Harold, looking up towards heaven, exclaimed "May the Lord now decide between William and me, and may he pronounce which of us has the right."'

The *Carmen* says the message was delivered somewhere in the forest before the battle, but the result is the same. 'Harold, his face distorted, throwing back his head, said to the envoy, "Return, you fool! Tomorrow with the Lord as arbiter of the kingdom, the rightful claimant will appear. The holy hand of the Lord will deal justly." '

One has to be doubtful of Norman stories about English people, but this one is an exception; for the monk's duty was to ride straight back to Hastings with Harold's answer, and the answer was a matter of prime importance to William and his councillors. I think one must believe at least that Harold was shocked by what the monk had told him. The chaplain merely explained that he was afraid and 'blinded by his lust for dominion'. Yet there is obviously something missing. There was nothing in the message the chaplain quoted that could have made Harold afraid, nothing new to surprise him, nothing of any importance he had not often heard before.

There was only one thing at that moment that could have come as a shock to him; but that one thing would indeed have been a devastating shock. I suggest it was at this eleventh hour that Harold was told (either in William's message, or by the monk himself, or by his own monk who had returned from Hastings) that William was fighting under the papal banner, that he was wearing on his finger the holy relic of St Peter and suspended round his neck the very relics on which Harold had sworn the oath in Normandy, even that William or his Bishop Odo was bearing a papal bull of Harold's excommunication. It was now he learned that he had already been judged and found guilty by the papal court, in his absence, without his knowledge, and without a word in his defence.

In itself, this is only inference. But it has one piece of direct confirmation: the *Roman de Rou* says what the chaplain does not say – that Harold was told, in this exchange of messages, that he and his followers had been excommunicated. So at least it is an inference worth following up; and if one follows it, it gathers more supporting evidence and leads to explanations of much that has been obscure.

First, it seems quite certain that if he had not heard of the papal judgement before, he heard of it now: his own envoy could not have spent a night at William's headquarters without discerning that the Normans thought of themselves as crusaders and learning the reason why.

Secondly, there is every sign that neither he nor anyone in England had heard of it before. It was not a thing that could have been shrugged off and disregarded during that summer by Harold himself, or the English church, or the English people. Yet Harold, all through the summer and through the march to York, seems perfectly confident and perfectly in command: the old oath may still have been on his conscience, but if it was he kept it to himself. The church and the army seem to have supported him without the slightest hesitation: they could not and would not have done so if they had known that the Pope had judged him in the wrong, if they suspected he was under a papal interdict that excluded him from the means of God's grace, or if they thought the same sentence might fall on his followers. Even at Waltham two or three days before, the canons could scarcely have ministered to a man under such a sentence.

Nor is it impossible or even unlikely that the news of the judgement had been kept out of England until then. A court that did not trouble to hear the defendant would hardly have troubled to send a special envoy to tell him its decision: it would have relied on the successful claimant to deliver it. During the summer, the decision had been well known in Normandy; but England was cut off from the continent. And if William understood the strength of the weapon the Pope had given him, he was wise to keep it until the moment when it could do most harm. I do doubt, though, that Harold and his followers had really already been excommunicated: more likely they were threatened with that solemn punishment if they refused to accept the papal judgement and surrender the crown. It may even have been that the Norman church assumed that would be the punishment and blew it up into a *fait accompli*: but true or false, it was terribly damaging at that moment, because there was no time to question it.

After that fateful day in London – it was Monday or Tuesday, 9 or 10 October – reports of Harold's behaviour are different. They are also Norman in origin, but they do not have the element of propaganda one learns to recognize, nor are they things a Norman could invent; and they are accepted by two respectable later writers, Ordericus Vitalis and William of Malmesbury. Harold's younger brother Gyrth emerges from obscurity, and the oath comes openly under discussion again.

When Harold told his brothers, as he had told the monk, that he was going to march at once to battle, Gyrth offered to go instead. He gave three reasons, and all of them seem good. First, he said Harold was too exhausted to march again so soon: second that Harold was bound to William by the oath and Gyrth was not, and whether the oath was valid or not it was a weakness in battle. Thirdly, if Harold lost and was killed in battle, the kingdom was lost; but if Gyrth fought and lost, Harold was free to raise a second army and fight again – and of course if Gyrth fought and won, all was well. He also made another strategic suggestion. While he himself fought at Hastings, Harold should empty the whole of the countryside behind him, block the roads, burn the villages and destroy the food: so, even if Gyrth was beaten, William's army would starve in the wasted countryside as winter came on.

That advice was intelligent and brave, a plan that could have defeated William. But Harold rejected it and insisted on going himself and going at once. Ever since, he has been accused of two strategic mistakes: one, of fighting before his whole army was assembled, and the other of assembling it too close to the enemy.

I think it is usually presumptuous to say that generals of the past made blunders: one seldom knows the information and experience they acted on, or the stresses that impelled them. But it is fair enough when people said it at the time, and the first of these criticisms of Harold was being made soon after the event. Even the Anglo-Saxon Chronicle points it out, and Florence of Worcester in 1118 says that if he had waited he could have had three times as many men.

The second criticism, of the place he chose to assemble, seems less valid. The place was actually on the watershed where the road came out of the Hastings triangle. There was an obvious reason for the choice: beyond that place there were two roads to London, and if he assembled farther away he could not be certain of intercepting William. It was certainly too near to be safe: it was open to attack at any moment William cared to choose. But this was not a mistake if Harold expected and intended to fight as soon as he arrived there, and there is every evidence that he did.

But having agreed that it was a strategic mistake to try to fight a final battle so soon, one has to ask why he did it. It was not just stupidity: he had never been stupid. It was not that he had failed to think of a better plan: Gyrth had proposed one. It might, of course, have been simply that he was sick or tired out, and perhaps depressed by his part in his brother's death. But much the most likely cause, I suggest, was the sudden revelation of the papal judgement.

This meant he was not merely defying William, he was defying the Pope. It was doubtful whether the church, the army and the people would support him in that defiance: at best, they would be bewildered and half-hearted. Therefore, since a battle had to be fought, it must be fought at once, without a day's delay, before the news leaked out. After that, if the battle was won, would be time to debate the Pope's decision, explain that the trial had been a travesty, query it, appeal against it, or simply continue to defy it.

Perhaps one may venture a little further in imagining the effect of this revelation on Harold's mind. Gyrth and his other friends (if one may guess) might try to reassure him, tell him again and again the papal decision was false, if only because the Pope had never heard the English side of the story. Yet could a Christian readily believe the papal court had been so blatantly unjust? Harold's own confidence in himself, his cause, his very right to be king, can only have been shaken to its foundation. Gyrth's proposal had offered a logical way to victory. But in a medieval mind, events could go beyond the logic of strategy. This had become a private matter of conscience. There was one higher appeal, to the judgement of God himself, and Harold could only surrender himself to that judgement: 'May the Lord now decide between William and me.' He had been challenged to meet for the final decision and he could not evade it; in order that God might declare his judgement, he was obliged to accept the challenge in person.

He left London in the morning of 12 October. A few friends came with him who knew what had happened and still believed in him: Gyrth and his brother Leofwine, his nephew Hakon whom he had rescued from Normandy, two canons from Waltham already nervous at the miracle they had seen, two aged and respected abbots who carried chain mail to wear above their habits, and – perhaps at a distance – Edith Svanneshals the mother of his sons. He led the army, who did not know, the remains of his house-carls and what-ever men of the fyrd had already gathered in London. The northern earls had been expected with contingents, but they had not come and he could not wait. He rode across London Bridge again and this time down the Dover road to Rochester, and then by the minor Roman road that plunged due south through the Andredeswald – the forest now yellow with autumn and the road already covered by fallen leaves. The men of Kent and Sussex were summoned to meet at an ancient apple tree that stood at the junction of the tracks out-side the enclave of Hastings. Harold reached that meeting place late on Friday 13, ready to face his judgement; and even while the army was forming for battle, if one may further believe the *Roman de Rou*, the terrible rumour was starting to spread that the King was excommunicated and the same fate hung over any man who fought for him.

Hastings

October 14

The Battle of Hastings has been fought on paper innumerable times, but strictly military accounts of it have always had to leave some mysteries unsolved. One source of the mysteries is that the early accounts are entirely one-sided. Within the lifetime of the men who fought, nothing was recorded on the English side. So one can only see the English army from the point of view of men who attacked it: one cannot know what happened inside its ranks. Moreover, the historians on William's side were not writing dry and factual narratives, they were telling exciting stories, each for a receptive audience of his own: Guy for the French, the chaplain for the Norman admirers of William, and the tapestry designer for the illiterate majority who preferred a strip-cartoon to a written page.

But I think one can come a little nearer a solution of the mysteries if one remembers the states of mind of the leaders, and so before I re-tell the well-known story I want to glance again at the events that brought William and Harold to their final meeting.

William was there through his own supreme effort of will, aided by a most extraordinary run of luck. By then he must have recognized the chances that had kept him in Normandy, through one delay after another, all the time when Harold was ready for him – and then had blown him safely across the Channel so late in the year, a fortnight after the equinox, at the one and only moment when Harold was not ready. But of course he did not think of it as luck: it was God's direct answer to his prayers. He also had the blessing of the Pope. That may have been marred for him when he remembered the trickery that had won it. But everything had happened to make him believe his cause was just in the sight of God; and I suppose that people who firmly believe in divine intervention must still come to the same conclusion. When Harold's army was sighted, he can only have been on the crest of a wave of self-righteous confidence that he probably never achieved again in his life.

Harold had started the year with the same sincere belief in the justice of his cause, and every bit of luck had gone against him, every coincidence of the two invasions. The objects of his prayers are not recorded as William's are. But if like him he prayed for victory, he saw nothing but added trials put in his way. Just before the battle, I believe, he was suddenly told that the head of the church had already judged him and inflicted the most solemn punishment: so that he waited that day in resignation for the final judgement of God, already prepared to believe he had been wrong.

The field of Hastings is partly covered now by the buildings of the abbey William founded as a penance for the slaughter, and by the town that grew up round it; but the features of the battlefield can still be plainly seen. It is the narrowest part of the watershed that leads out of the triangle William had overrun. The streams that lead to the River Brede in the east and the vanished harbour of Bulverhythe in the south-west are here not more than a quarter of a mile apart, and they run in steep little valleys that an army could not easily cross. The road from Hastings over this narrow divide rises first to a gentle summit named Telham Hill and then to another, a mile and a half beyond, named Caldbec Hill. In the dip between the two, a short ridge crosses the watershed at right angles. There was a

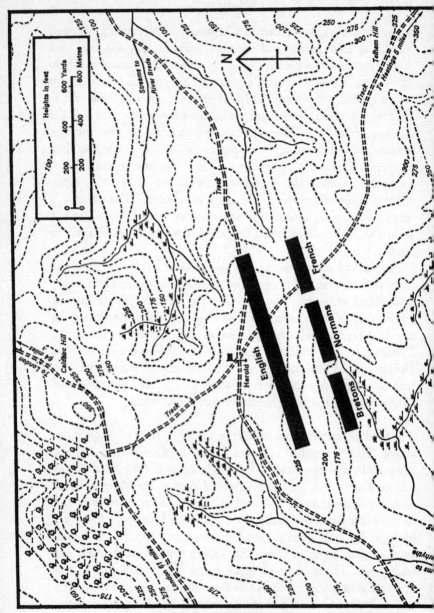

The Battle of Hastings

local lane or track along the top of that ridge, and to the south of it a shallow marshy valley that had the name of Santlache. The apple tree where Harold's army met was on Caldbec Hill, and the place he chose to defend was the cross-ridge rising out of the Santlache valley. All of it then was empty and uninhabited.*

Given that a defensive battle had to be fought, this was a very good position which Harold or some other expert must have noticed long before. The cross-ridge is eight hundred yards long; its ends are protected by the steep valleys, and it cuts right across the only road out of Hastings. It rises sixty feet above the lowest point on the road, and about a hundred and fifty above the bottom of the marshy valley. The slope of it varies: it is not very steep anywhere on the south side, not more than one in fifteen, but steep enough to give defenders the upper hand. Part of the slope may have been cultivated then, but the top of the ridge was open heath and the edge of the forest was at Caldbec Hill.

It has a peculiar likeness to the position Wellington chose at Waterloo – the gentle ridge with a lane along the top, the muddy valley, the main road cutting across it and the forest in the rear – but it is all on a miniature scale, one-quarter the length and depth of the field of Waterloo. Harold, like Wellington, set his battle head-quarters on the crossroads where the lane and the main road inter-sected; and the battle itself, one may add, was an equally near-run thing.

Estimates of the numbers of men on each side have mainly been based on the numbers that could possibly have been crammed into such a small battlefield. Standing shoulder to shoulder, one thousand men would stretch from end to end of the ridge, and five hundred horsemen riding stirrup to stirrup would be hard pressed to attack them in line. Many military experts have worked it out, and they do not differ much. The average of their findings is that William had seven or eight thousand men – three thousand horsemen, one thousand archers and the rest as infantry – and that Harold had very

* The Normans or French adapted this Anglo-Saxon name to Senlac or Sanguelac, Lake of Blood, and used it in later years as a name for the battle. But the name was not used before 1140, when Ordericus Vitalis seems to have invented it. All the earlier chroniclers, English or Norman, called it the Battle of Hastings.

slightly more. Neither side had kept any troops in reserve, but William may have had another two thousand assorted non-combatants and men who were left to guard the ships at Bulver-hythe and Pevensey. Even with these numbers, about one-sixth of the wilder contemporary claims, Harold's army would have been standing in a rank that was eight men deep, and one of William's problems, especially with his horsemen, would have been sheer congestion. Most men, to get at an enemy, would have had to elbow their way through the crowds of their friends.

Florence of Worcester, confirming the *Roman de Rou*, says that many men deserted from Harold's army, or at least went away again before the battle began. But he gives a different reason: not that they had heard of the excommunication, but that they thought the field of battle was too narrow – in other words, that the army was big enough without them.

The top of that ridge must indeed have been crowded the evening before while the army prepared to spend the October night in the open, scavenging for sticks, building what fires they could, eating the unattractive remains of whatever food they had brought, shouting greetings to unexpected friends, telling stories and talking, like any army, about anything except the impending battle. They were the last army in history that was homogeneous: they were not divided into separate arms, cavalry, infantry and artillery or archers. All of them were the same, except that some were better armed than others. Their weapons were battle-axes, swords and spears; javelins and smaller axes that were made to be thrown; and among the poorer men, stones tied to sticks which could be thrown a long way and probably did a lot of damage for such a simple device. History has tended to divide these men, with the house-carls as a professional core and the rest as raw levies or ignorant yokels. But that exaggerates the extremes. Most of them were raw, in that none had ever fought in a battle before, except the survivors of Stamford Bridge and perhaps a few old hands from Harold's expeditions in Wales. But most of them were members of the fyrd of the southern shires who had spent the summer preparing to fight, and had at least thought out the way they would do it and provided themselves with weapons. No doubt there were some from the villages round about who turned up to help and had not much idea what to do; but their numbers must have been small, and these were probably the kind of men who went away again as Florence of Worcester said.

There is no sign of organization in this throng. Nobody, for example, was separated out and told to form a reserve. But probably they did not expect to be ordered about. What they had to do was fairly simple – to stop the Norman bastard coming up the slope – and the way they expected to do it was very much an individual matter, every soldier fighting single-handed. So as each group of friends or neighbours arrived on the ridge, it only needed to find a place for itself among the crowd, as near as it could to somebody else's fire. The Normans said the English spent the night in drinking and singing raucous songs, while they themselves spent it in prayer. Perhaps they did, but it was a story often told when accounts of battles were written by bishops and monks.

As ever on the eve of battle, there is the mystery of why men were willing to kill and be killed. Armies, of course, have often fought for causes that were pure delusion, and the motives of William's soldiers were mixed and unreal. Some may have thought they were fighting a holy war to punish sinners. Some, but surely a few, may have fought in personal loyalty to William, and have been ready to die for what he thought was his right. Some, especially the knights, fought like the Norsemen for the pleasure of fighting. But the only real motive, overlying these others, was the thought of booty, the land and riches and power that William had promised them.

The English had a much more direct and comprehensible cause. They did not want a foreign king. They wanted the right to choose their own king in their own way, and to be ruled by the system they themselves had created. They wanted to stop a foreign army ravaging their villages. They wanted England to be English: they were defending their homes.

Harold himself was encamped that night in the middle of his mass of men, alone with his doubt. It seems to me perfectly clear that he was not surprised by William's attack, as many military historians have said. On the contrary, he had chosen his position and taken it before William could stop him, and he expected to fight the next day. One account of the challenge they had exchanged says the date, that Saturday, had been agreed. And he could not possibly have meant to keep the army waiting where it was, on top of a barren ridge in mid-October with no resources of food except half a dozen villages, some already despoiled, along the forest edge. Nor is it likely he meant to leave the strong position, march into the Hastings triangle and fight on ground that William chose. Nor can it be said he was unready. He needed a larger army for the defence of England, but not for the immediate battle: there were plenty of men to defend that ridge, if anything too many, and he was as ready as he would ever have been. His error was in the concept that this was to be the only and final battle, when God would declare his judgement – and not, as it might have been, the mere beginning of a long campaign.

When Harold's army was sighted, William called in his men from their foraging expeditions and ordered a march at dawn. During the night, according to Guy of Amiens, more envoys were sent with messages by both sides. It was an accepted custom to send superfluous messages just before a battle, not because the messages or the answers mattered, but simply to spy on the enemy's arrangements and find out his plans. Harold's envoys came back to report that William was coming in the morning, and also that a surprising number of the other army seemed to be priests; but Harold knew the Normans' fashion of shaving the backs of their heads, and he was not deceived. One of William's envoys, in the early morning, said he had seen the royal standards in the middle of the English host. There were two, the Dragon of Wessex which was the nearest thing to a national emblem, and Harold's personal standard, which was called the Fighting Man. So William learned that Harold was there in person; and it was then that he swore he would build an abbey, if victory was granted, with its altar on the spot where the English standards stood.

The date is agreed by all the chroniclers except one: it was the day of Calixtus the Pope in the church's calendar, or in the Julian

calendar *secundo Idus Octobris*, both of which were 14 October.
But as the Julian calendar was six days wrong by the seasons, 14
October then is now the day called 20 October. Sunrise was therefore about half past six, and by then William's army was ready to
march the five or six miles to Harold's ridge.

It was one of the conventions of early battle-reporting that
commanders should make inspiring speeches to their armies.
Obviously nobody could really make a speech to an army, and the
chaplain rather gave the game away. He wrote: 'Nobody has
reported to us in detail the short harangue with which on this
occasion the Duke increased the courage of his troops, but we do not
doubt it was excellent' – and he went straight on to quote the
speech at great length word for word. According to him, the Duke
delved far into Norman history, recalled triumphant battles, derided the English and once again promised honour and riches as the
rewards of victory. A later account says the knights were so excited
that they rushed impetuously off before he had finished and left him
speaking alone. Others also attribute a speech to Harold, which in
the nature of things they could not have known at all; but it was
less loquacious, and only reminded the army to keep its ranks close
against attack.

William's column on the narrow track must have been miles in
length: the rear of it had hardly started when the head came down
the slope of Telham Hill and into sight of the English, already
standing in their battle line. It halted while the knights put on their
coats of mail. William put his on back to front, but laughed off the
evil omen. They remounted and the column moved again. The
English, unmoving, watched it come on and deploy to right and
left of the road, two hundred yards away in the bottom of the
valley, until the two armies stood face to face. The time is less
certain than the date. Like the landing at Pevensey, it was said the
battle began at the third hour; but to judge by the length of the
march and the time such an army would take to deploy, it must have
been ten or eleven o'clock before they could begin.

William's army was a far more complex organization than Harold's.

It was in three divisions. The centre was Norman, under the direct command of himself and the warlike Bishop Odo. The left division when it deployed was mainly from Brittany, Maine and Anjou, and it was commanded by a Breton count, Alan Fergant. The right division was French and Flemish under Count Eustace of Boulogne, the man whose futile rage in Dover fifteen years before had triggered the quarrel between the Normans and the House of Godwin; and that division also had a Norman contingent under Robert of Beaumont. So the Norman troops who had some allegiance to William were mainly in the centre, and the assorted mercenaries on the wings. Within each division there were groups of knights from the major baronies who had fought together before and had leaders of their own.

Each division had its three arms: in front the archers, armed with a short bow and unarmoured, some also with crossbows which fired a heavier bolt; next the foot-soldiers, mailed and carrying swords and pikes; and behind, the mounted knights, with swords and spears or lances, some with iron maces, helmeted and mailed down to their knees but riding horses which were unprotected. Above the metallic glitter the emblems of early chivalry were carried, the banners and pennants, and the papal banner at William's position in the centre.

As the armies stood ready, a minstrel or juggler named Taillefer, with an eye to posthumous fame, rode out alone from the Norman ranks singing and throwing his sword in the air and catching it, cantered across the valley and into the English line, and was said to have killed three men before he was killed himself. Then the archers advanced in line abreast. The English doubled their front rank to form the wall of overlapping shields that defended an army from missiles, and the archers loosed their first volley at fifty paces.

Battle was joined.

Since gunpowder, deafening noise has been the essence of battle; it is hard to imagine now that the Battle of Hastings was comparatively silent, with only the evil thud of weapons, the sounds of the horses' hoofs on the muddy ground, the snorts and neighs, the human cries of triumph or agony, and ordinary conversation. The

Normans charged into battle shouting 'God's help', '*Dex aïe*': the English official war-cries were 'God Almighty' and 'Holy Cross' – an invocation of the Rood of Waltham. In more homely fashion, they shouted 'Out! Out!' as they ejected intruders from their line, pronouncing it probably with what now would be known as a north-country accent. Nobody a mile away in the English country-side would have heard the battle at all.*

All through the centuries when armies fought in three arms, the ideal technique of attack remained the same: first by missiles, arrows or artillery, to weaken and confuse the enemy line, then by infantry to break it up, and finally, at a crucial moment, by cavalry to ride down and destroy the scattered ranks. William's army seems to have had this sequence in mind, but it was not co-ordinated: each arm arrived too soon, before the previous one had done its work. The arrows did some damage, but the wall of shields took most of them. The mailed infantry came striding up and through the archers but the mass of the English line had not been touched, and before the infantry came to an arm's length they were halted by a hail of missiles thrown by the Englishmen behind the shield wall. When the cavalry came charging through, the line was far from broken. Horses jibbed at charging it, and house-carls man by man leaped forward out of line to find the space to swing their awful axes.

Englishmen had never met horsemen in battle, nor had the knights ever met such furious opposition. Especially, they had never met the battle-axe, and by all accounts they were horrified at the ghastly wounds it gave to men and horses. It was the knights who broke. In the left division among the Bretons, chaotic retreat began – or so said the Norman chaplain. Horsemen wheeling round to escape rode down through their infantry and archers and put them too to flight. In the marshy bottom of the valley, scores or hundreds

* The *Roman de Rou* explains rather charmingly for Norman-French readers:

> '*Olicrosse* sovent crioent,
> E *Godemite* reclamoent;
> *Olicrosse* est en engleiz
> Ke Sainte Croix est en franceiz,
> Et *Godemite* altretant
> Com en franceiz Dex tot poissant.'

of horsemen fell in a ditch – and the right wing of the English, irresistibly tempted, broke ranks and rushed down the hill to attack the knights where they struggled with their horses in the mud. A shouted rumour spread through the Norman army that the Duke was killed: the Norman division joined the retreat and then the French, but the rest of the English line stood where it was. William took off his helmet so that men would know him, and the chaplain said he 'thrust himself in front of those in flight, shouting at them and threatening them with his sword.' And he turned the disaster to success. Only the end of the English line had joined the pursuit. So it was isolated from the rest with its flank exposed, a scattered mass of men who had thrown off the close-ranked defence against cavalry. William saw this chance and rallied the Norman horsemen, and they rode round the English and cut them off. The Bayeux tapestry shows the slaughter, on and around a little hillock that can still be seen in the lower part of the valley.

It has often been said that this English counter-attack was a mistake by inexperienced troops in defiance of orders. So it probably was. But what went wrong was that only one end of the line advanced and the rest did not. There undoubtedly was a moment of very serious chaos in William's army, and if the whole English line had attacked at that moment it might have succeeded. Nobody now can tell: but the partial attack reveals the greatest of the mysteries of the day. For excepting these local sallies out of the line which were always fatal, the English army never moved. It never acted as if it had received a general order: it stood where it was all day, only shrinking in on itself as its numbers fell. It never made a concerted attack, nor in the end did it make a concerted retreat. Either Harold never gave a general order, or else it was never carried out.

This immobility astonished the Normans at the time, and it has puzzled people ever since. A position may be held by a static defence, but a battle cannot be won without attack – and the English needed to win, not merely to hold that ridge. The reasons why they stood still can only be surmised, but I have two suggestions that may have been interconnected.

The first is in Harold's state of mind. I would not press this too far, but the strangely passive battle he fought seems to fit a mood of fatalism, as if he scarcely fought for victory but simply awaited the expression of God's judgement. His behaviour at Stamford Bridge and Hastings was utterly different. Both battles were equally long and equally hard fought, between armies almost equally matched; but in the first he was always in attack, and in the second never. In the first, and in the whole episode of York, he undoubtedly inspired everyone; but in the second he left no evidence of leadership at all. He acted like a different man: something had changed him in the eighteen days between, and I have already suggested what it was.

The other reason I offer is that the scope of battle and the size of armies had suddenly outgrown the English system of command. So far as one knows, nobody in the Anglo-Saxon world had ever tried before to command an army of eight thousand men in battle, and I doubt if it was possible to do it effectively. William on horseback could gallop from end to end of the field, and he had mounted aides who could bring him reports and carry orders quickly to his sub-ordinate commanders. Moreover, his army was in nine quite separate units, each of a manageable size – three divisions each with its three arms. He could and he certainly did make use of his skill to change the course of the battle.

But Harold was on foot, mailed and carrying the sword and battle-axe; and where he was on foot it seems unlikely that he had a staff that was mounted. Probably Gyrth and Leofwine each com-manded a part of the line, but the only known division of the army was such that its units – house-carls, thanes, fyrd and villagers – were scattered all over the field. It seems Harold never moved from his post on the crossroads: he was there at the beginning and still there at the end, and no Norman reported having seen him in the battle-line, though William and every knight with an eye to glory were searching for him. How could he have controlled a line eight hundred yards long and eight men deep? How much of it could he have seen, over the heads of the crowd? How long would an order have taken to reach the ends of it – an aide on foot shoving his way through the ranks to search for some captain who was also on foot? Could even a bugle call in those days – something like a hunting horn – have carried such a distance among the other sounds of battle? In retrospect it seems there were several moments in the battle when the English might have counter-attacked as a whole and carried everything before them in the kind of hand-to-hand and free-for-all fighting they excelled at. But if this was so, then either Harold failed to see the chances, or else his orders failed to reach the men.

In short, it may be that in the simple English system it was possible to order an attacking battle, as at Stamford Bridge, or a defensive battle as at Hastings, and the individual soldiers would go on doing what they had been told until they died. But once the fighting began, it was almost impossible for a commander on foot, with an army of such a size, to change the direction of the battle from defence to attack – and harder still to see and seize a fleeting opportunity. If Harold had been the man he was at Stamford Bridge he might have found a way of doing it. He might have been out in front where men could see him, at whatever risk to himself – as his brothers were, and as William was. But he was behind the line, and most of the men in front, one can only suppose, stood facing death all day without a word of encouragement or command from the King they were fighting for.

There must have been a long pause after the first attack. No chronicle mentions it, but even the fiercest battle is not continuous. The Normans needed time to sort themselves out. The archers needed a new supply of arrows; archers often re-armed by pulling the enemy's arrows out of the ground and the corpses, but this time there were none. And the English needed to go out and retrieve their assorted missiles, which was perfectly safe when the Normans were back where they started.

The next episode was exactly like the first, except that it happened at the other end of the line. The French and Flemish division attacked, just as the Bretons had before; they were repulsed and retreated, the end of the English line broke ranks and chased them, and again were counter-attacked by horsemen before they could go back. But this time, the chaplain said the Duke had ordered a deliberate feigned retreat to tempt the English out. The claim has been treated with suspicion. 'Tactical retreat' is a phrase that has been used so often in the centuries since to disguise the fact that somebody ran away; and some experts can hardly believe that such a manoeuvre could have been ordered and carried out in the midst of a fight. Nor could it have been if William had suddenly thought of it as a brilliant new idea. But this was only the chaplain's implication. It was not a new idea: it was a well-established stratagem in Byzantine armies, especially recommended in a famous handbook of tactics written by the Emperor Leo about the year 900. William had studied tactics all his life and, illiterate though he may have been, he must have known of this book; and Norman knights in Sicily had actually tried the trick. So I think it is not impossible that groups of them had rehearsed it and could carry it out on a signal.

Moreover, Guy of Amiens puts these events in a different and more plausible order. He says the feigned retreat was the first event in the battle, coming before the rout, not after it. And in one of his most scandalous passages, he says it was the French ('versed in stratagem and skilled in warfare') who carried out the delicate manoeuvre, and it was the Normans who fled in uncontrolled panic ('their shields covered their backs'). It was no wonder the Normans disliked the *Carmen*.

Some time in this early part of the battle, both Harold's brothers were killed, Gyrth and Leofwine. Guy says that Gyrth encountered William himself and threw a javelin which missed the Duke but killed his horse: and the Duke, on foot, 'rushed upon the young man like a snarling lion and hewed him limb from limb, and shouted "Take the crown you have earned from us!"' – an enigmatic phrase that seems to suggest he thought he was killing Harold. Evidently, the brothers were both in the thick of the fighting, and it is tempting to put two and two together and guess that they commanded the wings of the army and led the two abortive advances – and perhaps had a moment of surprise and anger before they died when they saw that Harold's centre had not followed their lead but was standing still and leaving them isolated.

Those two advances, and perhaps a third of the same kind, may have killed or put out of action two or three thousand Englishmen. Their line shrank in length. But it was still unbroken and showed no sign of breaking. The Norman infantry seem to have failed to come to grips with it at all, and they vanish from all accounts of the later part of the battle. Both the *Carmen* and the chaplain tell of terrible fights between the English on foot and the knights on horse-back, and William, as was only natural, plays the major part in them. Unhorsed, he called to a knight of Maine to dismount for him, but the frightened fellow refused: William turned on him and furiously seized him by the nose-piece of his helmet, threw him head over heels to the ground and took his horse. That horse was also killed. Eustace of Boulogne, the leader of the Frenchmen, came to the rescue of the Duke and gave him his horse, and took another from one of his followers; and from then on, in the French account, 'the count and the duke joined forces and renewed the battle to-gether wherever the clashing arms glittered most brightly. By the swords of both the field was cleared of English and many fled, staggering and exhausted. As the waning wood falls to the stroke of the axe, so the forest of Englishmen was brought to nothing.'

The chaplain allowed no rivals to his hero who, he said, excelled all others in bravery and skill and dominated the battle. 'At the mere sight of this wonderful and redoubtable knight, many enemies lost heart before they received a scratch. Thrice his horse fell under him; thrice he lept upon the ground; thrice he quickly avenged the death of his steed. His sharp sword pierced helmets, shields and armour.' And one may well believe that faith in divine approval, added to his natural martial courage, made him a formidable fighter.

Nevertheless, this battle of horsemen versus footmen was evenly matched: if it had not been, it could not have lasted so long. It went on all the afternoon. One must picture the awful scene of slashing and stabbing all along the English line and extending a few yards in front of it, where Englishmen stepped out to give themselves space to swing their weapons and left the mass of the army standing stolidly behind them. But of course there were pauses when the horsemen withdrew to rest and reorganize, and it was probably in the pauses that the Normans began to wear the English down. For whenever the horsemen were out of the way, the archers began again. The alternation of missiles and cavalry was always a hard ordeal because there was very little active defence against it: the best defence was to stand still and close the gaps where friends had fallen dead. The English suffered that trial at Hastings just as they did with their allies on the afternoon of Waterloo. But at Hastings there was an added hardship: the Norman arrows had a range of a hundred yards, but the English could hardly throw their missiles a quarter as far. So when the Normans withdrew they could rest in safety, but the English had no rest.

Not even this treatment shook the English line. The Normans watched it with surprise and grudging admiration: the only movement in it, they said, was the movement of the men who fell, and those who lay wounded unable to crawl away through the crowd behind them. It was even said the line was so tightly packed that dead men could not fall down but were held upright by the press of living men around them.

If this was so, something had gone badly wrong; the repeated reports of the shrinking and congestion of the line are another mystery. A line that was eight men deep would not be expected to shrink in length whatever happened; men from behind would come forward to fill the gaps in front. The only plausible explanation is that the front rank, the shield-wall, was formed entirely by house-carls, and that they were determined to keep it that way. It is hardly credible that nobody in all the ranks behind them was willing to step forward; but the house-carls were trained together, and they might have preferred to have another tried companion on each side of them, and even have elbowed out a man who offered to join them. So as they shrank together, like a thin outer rind or skin, the ranks behind them may have grown thicker rather than thinner, until the army was so compressed that most of its men were helpless to fight at all.

William, or the archers themselves, observed that they were offered a most unusual target. Most of their well-aimed arrows were taken on the shield-wall, but behind it was a solid mass of men. They began to shoot on a high trajectory, so that their arrows fell on the heads of the men behind.

It became a battle of attrition, a question whether one side would break from weakness and exhaustion, or whether the night would come to put a stop to it; and it was still in the balance at five o'clock when the sun was setting.

The shrinking of the line left the ends of the ridge unguarded, and in the evening light some knights rode up to the top of it, first at the western end and then in the east. So they were able to penetrate behind the line and fight on level ground, and the English had to defend three sides of the dwindling area round the battle standards. Seeing them there, William's soldiery on the slopes below began to hunt for booty and strip the dead of their mail. But the fighting on top was more ferocious than ever. From somewhere far off, William saw Harold himself 'fiercely hewing to pieces the Normans who were besetting him.' He called Eustace to help him and they rode off with two other knights to seek the final encounter.

It is always too easy in military history to say what should have been done; but calmly looking back, it seems there must have been a moment which came and passed when Harold might have made a fighting retreat to the forest edge which offered safety very close behind him. But perhaps no commander in the middle of that warring throng could have chosen the moment; perhaps the manoeuvre itself was too dangerous; perhaps there was still no means of giving the order. At all events, he did not try to extricate the surviving army, or to escape his own impending death. Perhaps again, he did not want to live to fight again; or perhaps he was blinded before he thought the tactical moment had come.

The manner of Harold's death is the last of the mysteries of Hastings. For nine hundred years, people have believed he was shot in the eye by one of the arrows falling out of the evening sky. The story first appears, or seems to appear, in the Bayeux tapestry; it was first recorded in writing in the otherwise unimportant account of the battle by Baudri of Bourgueil in 1099. Neither of the early chronicles mentions the arrow-wound: the *Carmen* describes exactly how William and his three companions killed the King, and the chaplain says nothing at all about how he died. Recent critics have suggested that the man in the tapestry who seems to be pulling an arrow out of his eye is not meant to be Harold, and that Baudri was the first of many historians to be deceived by it. But the story of the arrow was accepted by the Anglo-Norman chroniclers, and there is no positive reason to discard the ancient belief. The stories are not contradictory.

Guy of Amiens in the *Carmen* relates the bloody deed of William and the knights with obvious approval. The chaplain would certainly have relished, if he could, the poetic justice that Harold should have died at William's hand. But before he wrote, I suggest, the Normans had learned what the English already knew: that Harold was wounded before the knights arrived, and it was not a gallant but an ignoble story that four men had to take part in killing one man who was already blind. The tapestry seems to record the arrow and one of the blows that was struck by a knight, but does not say William was there. Henry of Huntingdon says that Harold was hit in the eye, and that then a crowd of horsemen burst in through the ranks and killed him. William of Malmesbury suggests he had already died of the arrow-wound when the knights came and cut him to bits. Edward Freeman in 1869, the doyen of comparatively modern writers on the conquest, misread the *Carmen*, apparently on purpose, to try to conceal that William took any part in the barbarous deed.

I therefore believe one may both accept the story of the arrow and the story that Guy of Amiens told before the Normans knew it was better forgotten. They are both as probably true as any of this history. This then was the horrible means of Harold's death. After William saw him fighting from afar, he was struck by the arrow. It did not kill him at once, but a man who was shot in one eye could not see with the other. He stood or crouched or lay there, a blind man with the battle raging round him, waiting for the blow he knew must come. William and Eustace rode in on him: the others were Hugo of Ponthieu, the son of the man who had imprisoned him, and a knight with the honoured name of Giffard. They hacked him to pieces. One of them stabbed him in the chest, another cut off his head, another disembowelled him, and the last cut off his leg at the thigh and carried it away. William of Malmesbury says the Duke thought the last of these deeds was ignominious and dismissed the man from the army: the translators of the *Carmen* suggest the Latin word for thigh was a euphemism.

It was not a quick or merciful death: while Harold was blind, there was time for the thought to penetrate his pain that God had declared his judgement.

London

October 15 - December 25

I have not tried to make excuses for Harold, only to find the reasons for what he did. I think one has to sympathize with a man so bludgeoned by fate, and with a man who is mainly remembered in history for what was said about him by the propagandists of foreign enemies. All the evidence is that they were wrong, that everyone who knew him liked him, and that he was an inspiring leader until the last few days of his life. I also think there is not much doubt he would have won if every bit of luck had not gone against him – and even without the luck he would still have won if something, which I believe was the Pope's decision, had not destroyed his confidence in himself.

But still, it remains a fact that he failed in one of the duties of a king, the duty to defend the realm. Many far worse men have reigned in England since, but even the worst of them did not lose the kingdom to a foreign invader. If he had been a less likeable person, perhaps he would have been a more successful king. Through that failure a whole generation of English people suffered death, desolation, robbery and bewilderment. They were divided in their reaction to disaster. Some blamed Harold, not for losing the battle but for whatever sins had turned the judgement of God against him. But others remembered him with affection. Some fought against the disaster for years, but many accepted it with the resignation I have suggested Harold felt, and believed they also had incurred the anger of God by racial or individual sins. This confusion began as soon as the battle ended.

The end came quickly when Harold died and his standards were seen to fall. The survivors scattered and retreated to the forest; but among them was an unknown leader who rallied some for a final stand on the forest edge. There is a steep ravine just north of where the apple tree stood on Caldbec Hill, and the Normans named it Malfosse, the Evil Ditch; for a crowd of horsemen riding down the slope of the hill in the dusk fell into it and were slaughtered by Englishmen lined up on its other bank. Eustace of Boulogne distinguished himself again. The *Carmen* says he led the pursuit; the chaplain says he fled from this affair and met the Duke and told him he must retreat – and as he said the cowardly words something or somebody hit him so hard in the back that blood ran out of his nose and mouth and he had to be carried away. The Duke, 'superior to all fear and dishonour', continued the advance. But not for long: a moonless night was falling, the enemy disappeared among the trees, and when it was dark William rode back to Harold's position on the ridge. He ordered a space to be cleared by dragging aside the corpses, and there in the stench of death he spent the night.

Inevitably, stories soon began about Harold's body. It was said his old mother, Godwin's widow, sent a messenger who offered to buy it from William for its weight in gold. She was perhaps the most tragic of the shadowy figures of 1066, for four of her five surviving sons were killed within a month, while the youngest was still imprisoned in Normandy. William refused her request, apparently angry that a Godwin should ask him for anything. Also, there was a practical problem: all the English bodies had been robbed and stripped of their armour and were lying naked in heaps, and nobody knew which was Harold's. In the saddest and most macabre scene of all, Edith Svanneshals was brought to search for the horribly disfigured and dismembered corpse. She recognized it by marks that only a lover would have known.

William had the pieces wrapped in a purple cloth and took them back to Hastings, and insisted they should be buried under a heap of stones on top of a cliff of the shore that Harold had defended. He entrusted the job to a man named William Malet, who was half-English and half Norman and had been a companion of Harold; and Malet put a stone on the grave with the epitaph:

'By command of the Duke, you rest here a King, O Harold,
That you may be guardian still of the shore and sea.'

This strange ceremony was a purely pagan Viking rite. The chaplain seems so embarrassed at the Duke's behaviour that he passes it off as a mockery of Harold, a sick kind of joke. But the *Carmen* does not. 'The Duke,' it continues, 'lamenting with his people over the buried bones, gave alms to the poor of Christ. He discarded the name of Duke, and the King being thus interred he assumed the royal title and departed.' One is left to guess what bond the burial signified between William and his victim, what old pre-Christian magic he felt he had to propitiate.

However, the records of Waltham Abbey say the two canons who had followed Harold to Hastings also begged William to let them take the body for Christian burial, and that he relented and they took it to Waltham.

All this was probably near the truth, but not many people have ever believed the final inevitable legend: that Edith Svanneshals was mistaken and the body finally buried at Waltham was another man's: Harold had been carried away by friends when he was wounded, and lived to a very old age. A more subtle version suggests that Edith could not find the body but chose one at random, so that the Normans should not suspect that Harold might still be alive. The story is told in the *Vita Haroldi* written by a monk of Waltham itself in 1216. First, it is said, Harold went to Denmark to ask for refuge with his cousin King Swein, then he travelled on pilgrimage abroad; but when he was growing old he came back to

England and lived for ten years as a hermit in a cave in the cliffs of Dover. Then as an added penance he went to live unknown in Shropshire among the Welsh people he had fought in Edward's reign. He called himself Christian, and always wore a cloth over his face so that he had to be led like a blind man: nobody knew why. The author surmised that he thought he might be recognized or that he wanted to hide his wounds, but strangely he did not connect his story with the other, that Harold had lost his eye. Finally, as a very aged man, Harold lived, again as a hermit, in a cemetery chapel outside the walls of Chester, and there in his death-bed confession he told a priest who he was. It is one of those stories that could conceivably be true, but cannot conceivably be proved. One can only add that if it had been true, his long penance would have made a fitting sequel to his acceptance of judgement.

When the Normans had buried their dead they retreated to Hastings again. Nobody knows their casualties, but they must have been very severe, with large numbers of wounded demanding some kind of attention to save their lives. Military men, comparing this with later battles, have estimated that thirty per cent may have fallen, reducing the army to not much more than five thousand. And not only men: the trained war-horses must have suffered more than their riders, and they also were irreplaceable. Plenty of English ponies had been abandoned, so knights did not suffer the ignominy of walking; but they could not have fought a battle on untrained horses.

William himself must have found the next few weeks bewildering and astonishing. He had done what he said he would do: he had killed the usurper. He certainly knew by then that Tostig and Harald Hardrada were also dead. He was not only, as he believed, the true heir to the throne, but was also the only surviving claimant except the boy Edgar. In that sense, there seemed to be no opposition left. In military terms, on the other hand, his position was desperately weak: perhaps five thousand active men, very few effective horsemen, little hope of reinforcement, no retreat, no food unless he advanced to capture it, no winter quarters. The English had lost an army, but they still had enormous reserves, outnumbering his perhaps by ten to one.

So there were two alternatives he could expect. Either the country's leaders would begin to come in to submit to him and offer their allegiance: or else enormous armies were building up against him and might attack at any moment. But neither of these things happened: nothing happened at all. Harold's army had suddenly appeared, and its remnants suddenly vanished. The country again fell silent and enigmatic; the wall of forest, sodden and dripping now with the autumn mists, was empty again and deserted; no message, either hostile or submissive, came through it from the world beyond. He had to move, if only to find more food, but it needed a brave decision to march in such weakness into unknown country with winter coming on.

When he left the Hastings triangle, he crossed the battlefield among the Norman graves and unburied English corpses, but he did not take either of the roads to London: they both led through the forest, where traps and ambushes might have been laid at every turn. He went east by a minor Roman road round the head of Rye harbour, through Benenden, Tenterden and Ashford, and so to Dover. He sent a detachment to wreak his vengeance on the port of Romney, where the two lost ships of his fleet had landed and their crews had been put to death. The warning of the annihilation of Romney spread before him: Dover was one of the few towns in England already fortified, but its people surrendered without a fight. Nevertheless, the Normans burned it – and here was confirmation that William could not control his army's lust for booty and destruction. The chaplain said he was 'unwilling that those who had offered to surrender should suffer loss, and he gave them a recompense in money. He would have severely punished the men who had started the fire if their numbers and base condition had not prevented their detection.'

In Dover the army fell sick with gastro-enteritis, so badly that some were expected to die of it. They put it down to the food they were eating and especially the water they drank, for they had run out of wine. They were probably right, and it is a whimsical thought that if they had brought less wine they might have been out of action with diarrhoea and fever on the day of battle. William waited a week (the *Carmen* says a month), and added to the fortifications: if the worst came to the worst, Dover gave a chance of escape across the straits even in winter, and he probably brought up some of the ships from Pevensey. One-third of the army had to be left to recuperate. With the rest, he marched on towards Canterbury, and that city also surrendered. Then he fell sick himself, and halted for almost a month at a place the Normans called the Broken Tower, which has never been identified. That long halt may partly have been due to the illness, but partly also to indecision at the baffling silence.

By another coincidence, all the secular leaders left in England at this moment of crisis were very young. One can seldom find exactly when a man was born, but Earls Edwin and Morkere, as nearly as one can tell, were eighteen and seventeen. Waltheof of Huntingdon, the only other surviving earl, was not much over twenty. Edgar the remaining claimant to the throne was thirteen. Harold's three sons had no official rank and may not have been in London, but they fought against William not long after, and they were teen-agers. Of course there were plenty of older men, bishops and thanes and officials of every kind, to deluge them with conflicting and confusing advice; but these were the men, or boys, who had to make decisions and try to carry them out, and one cannot help feeling sorry for them.

The one thing everyone agreed about was that they did not want a foreign king. This even penetrated the biased mind of William's chaplain: 'Their chief desire,' he wrote, 'was to have as king not a stranger but a fellow-countryman.' The only one of the young men who could be chosen without offending the others was Edgar, the youngest of them all. A witena gemot was held, and Edgar was elected King. The earls promised they would fight for him; so did the people of London and the crews of Harold's ships which were still in the river. A sheriff named Esgar or Edegar came into prominence as a warlike leader: he had escaped from Hastings so badly wounded that he could not ride or walk but had to be carried round

London in a litter. The will existed to carry on the fight in the new King Edgar's name. So did the opportunity. The fyrd could have been called in from counties so far unaffected, more armies could have been mobilized, the Normans could have been overwhelmed in a series of battles or worn away by guerrilla attacks and ambushes on the march. William could still have been beaten. But his psychological weapons were working for him.

It was the bishops who first had doubts. Both the archbishops are said to have been in London, Stigand of Canterbury and Aldred of York; so – at least part of the time – were Wulfstan of Worcester, Harold's friend and advocate, and Walter of Hereford; and so, no doubt, was William of London, who was a Norman appointed by King Edward. These men were all of an older generation than the earls, old enough to be the new King's grandfathers. They had concurred in electing him, but with elderly prudence they delayed his coronation.

There is no record of the moral debate that must have gone on amongst them, but it is easy to see the strength of the arguments. The papal judgement was now confirmed as right in the eyes of God by Harold's defeat and death. But was this a judgement against Harold in person, for the broken oath and other private sins? Or was it a judgement in William's favour, which gave him a right above all others to be King – a right in spite of the wishes of the English people? If so, it must be accepted that the English as a whole had been guilty of sin. The concept of national sin was nothing new: popes in the past had pronounced anathema on entire nations. As news came in of the Normans' ravages, Edward's apocalyptic death-bed dream came back to mind: for the wickedness of the earls and churchmen, he had said, God had cursed the country; devils would come through the land with fire and sword and war. It had come true. The disaster of Hastings, the burning of towns and villages, the murder, rape and robbery, began to appear as a punishment: and since God's punishment was just, England must unawares have committed sins that deserved it. It began to seem a risky course for the church to encourage opposition to William, which might be judged to be opposition to the Pope or even to the will of God himself. The safe way was to preach repentance and submission.

The moral problem gave infinite scope for splitting hairs and weighing arguments, and it spread to more practical thoughts. People tried to guess at William's intentions. Would he be satisfied with killing Harold? Would he accept England's choice of young Edgar, with whom he had no quarrel? Was there a compromise to offer, some kind of division of power? These naïve suggestions had an evil effect on Edwin and Morkere. If they withdrew, they began to argue, would William not leave them alone in their distant earldoms and confirm them in office?

The bargain William and Lanfranc had made with Hildebrand and the Pope had been more successful than they could have foreseen. It had brought William more recruits, which was its prime intention. But it had also destroyed Harold's confidence and impelled him towards defeat – and now the echoes of it rotted the will of the English to fight for what they wanted.

From Canterbury the principal Roman road of England, Watling Street, ran straight to London. But William did not go that way. He took a very circuitous route, prowling round London like an animal that suspects a trap, and the whole of it can be followed in the Domesday record of destruction.

Yet this record still does not suggest the devastation was a deliberate policy. No doubt it was useful in creating fear, and no doubt he was satisfied to let it happen, knowing very well that he could not stop it without annoying his troops. But it looks like the normal destruction of a ruthless army on the march in conquered country: the devastated villages and manors are found in separate groups twenty-five miles apart – a day's march on alternate days, and a day's halt between each march to scavenge for food and enjoy the wanton pleasure of displaying power. When William used destruction as a policy, as he did in the years that followed, he did it much more thoroughly; he laid waste thousands of square miles of England so completely that they were uninhabited, and uninhabitable, for a generation after he had gone.

The trail of tragedy leads not along the Roman road from Canterbury but on the smaller, more devious Pilgrims' Way, which follows the escarpment of the North Downs and passes twenty-five miles south of London. The Broken Tower may have been somewhere on this road, perhaps at Maidstone where it crosses the river Medway, or near Sevenoaks where it crosses the Darenth. While William waited there, he sent out five hundred horsemen to test the defence of London. They camped at the village of Camberwell and demolished it, and rode on to the suburb of Southwark at the southern end of London Bridge. The London people crossed the bridge, fought them and were driven back. But the Normans did not try to force the bridge: they burned Southwark, and then rejoined the army.

To judge by the destruction, the main force waited at Nutfield, near the modern town of Redhill; and from there a larger detachment was sent to Winchester. That was a city of historic and sentimental importance, the ancient capital of Wessex and in the great days of Alfred and Knut the capital of England. Now with the rise of London it had become a kind of dower property, and it was held in 1066 by Queen Edith, Edward's widow and Harold's sister. She is said to have been the only important person in England who positively wanted William as King, and it was from her that he received the first offer of submission. About the same time that his detachment marched, a reinforcement of horsemen succeeded in crossing the Channel and landed at Fareham in Portsmouth harbour; and between them, with Edith's agreement, they took over the famous city. From there they marched north and met William again on the Thames. He used two places where ancient roads cross the river. The infantry, or most of it, crossed at Goring on the West Ridgeway. William himself and the cavalry went right up to Wallingford, the crossing of the Icknield Way, nearly fifty miles from London and only thirteen from Oxford. He waited there while his hungry troops assaulted the surrounding villages: and there, the first defector came from London.

Significantly, it was Stigand, Archbishop of Canterbury, the man who had been present at Edward's death and scoffed then at his prophetic dream. He was not only the senior prelate of the English church, but also of all men in England the one who could least afford to incur the Pope's displeasure. He was already suspect in the Normans' eyes because he had replaced the Norman Archbishop Robert, and because his appointment was considered uncanonical; and he knew very well that if the church of England could be said to have sinned, he would be counted as the principal sinner. Perhaps he had really persuaded himself that William's cause was just: perhaps, in the logic of those days, it could be right to award the crown to the instrument of God's vengeance. But perhaps he hoped to protect his own position; and if so he suffered the fate of appeasers all through the ages, for William threw him from power as soon as he dared.

The archbishop's desertion, the loss of Canterbury and Winchester, and horror at the trail of wreckage the Normans left behind them, were almost mortal blows to the Londoners' will to resist, but it still took a few weeks to die. William marched on along the Icknield Way to the north-east, still keeping his distance. He sent out detachments farther north to watch the Roman roads near Cambridge, St Neots and Stony Stratford; and in December, nearly two months after the battle, he came to the neighbourhood of Hertford, twenty miles due north of the city, and stopped again. He had marched three-quarters of a circle round it. On the way, he had sent out so many detachments and left so many garrisons at important places that the army that remained with him must have been tiny. It had no possible way of retreat and was almost absurdly vulnerable. To have used it to keep up a show of power must be reckoned one of the greatest bluffs in military history. Yet to this puny force, London and England surrendered, not in a fight but in morbid guilt and confusion. William had a good idea by then what was happening in the capital. He had heard of Edegar the crippled sheriff as the most warlike leader, perhaps the only man he still had to fear, and he sent him a very surprising secret proposition: that he himself should only be king in name, and would administer the kingdom under Edegar's direction. It was a stratagem of course, and it succeeded. Edegar (one has only the word of the *Carmen* for it) told nobody of the message but spoke to a meeting of the witan: they could not win by force, he now told them, and must try by guile. A messenger should be sent to deceive the Duke with words, to feign submission and a pact of peace; if the Duke demanded it, they should all offer him a counterfeit homage. So they would play for time.

The messenger was sent. 'But the fox can hardly be held by open snares,' the *Carmen* said, 'and this man was deceived by the Duke whom he sought to deceive; openly the Duke commended the message he had brought, but secretly derided it. He blinded the fool with gifts, promised him innumerable rewards and sent him back weighed down with gold.' The man returned to report that the Duke offered safety and peace and complied with all their demands: he was a greater king than David, more glorious than the sun, wiser than Solomon and more bountiful than Charlemagne – and the only thing to do if they wished to survive was to render him homage and give him his rightful crown.

This seems to have been the final straw that convinced them they had been wrong. A deputation went out to submit. The Anglo-Saxon Chronicle says it happened at Berkhamstead, but the Domesday evidence points to the village of Little Berkhamstead, which is farther east near Hertford. Here came the Archbishop of York, bringing with him other bishops, Edgar the young uncrowned king, Earls Edwin and Morkere, possibly Earl Waltheof, and 'all the great men of London.' 'They submitted from necessity,' the Chronicle said, 'when the greatest harm had been done. It was very imprudent that they had not done it sooner, since God, for our sins, would not better things for us. They gave hostages and swore oaths to him, and he promised them he would be a kind lord to them; and yet, even while they were there, the Normans were ravaging all that they passed over.'

It was no honest promise: he had already promised the spoils and lands of England to his invaders. He no more intended kindness than he intended to act as vassal of the Pope. But for the moment it deceived them, and they invited him to be king, saying that they were accustomed to serve a king – and thinking perhaps that it was as well to bind him by the oaths of kingship. He is said to have hesitated and consulted his army, because he wanted Matilda to be crowned with him and because the country was still unsettled – he had in fact scarcely conquered a tenth of it. But he let himself be persuaded, 'in the hope', the chaplain said, 'that after he had begun to reign, men would hesitate to rebel against him, or if they did so, would be more easily crushed.'

He was so free from opposition, the chaplain also said, that he might have occupied his leisure in hawking and hunting. Nevertheless he refused to enter London until his men had run up one of their forts inside the walls for his protection: it is supposed to have been on the site of the Tower of London. On Christmas Day he was crowned in Edward's abbey at Westminster: not by Stigand, but by Aldred, Archbishop of York, who had also crowned Harold. The ancient English rites were used again, with some minor changes and in a different order. The *Carmen*, which begins to give a detailed account of the ceremony, breaks off and ends abruptly in the middle of it: the last page of the only manuscript is missing – almost as if somebody destroyed it, for it may have related a scandalous story. The chaplain goes a little further. The congregation, he says, was asked to declare its approval (it had to be done twice, by a Norman bishop in French and by Aldred in English) and the people 'shouted their joyous assent. Those who for safety were keeping guard outside the abbey, being armed and mounted, thought that the shouting boded some ill, and so without reason they started to set fire to the city.' Ordericus Vitalis takes the story further still. Smoke drifted into the church and the uproar outside could be heard. The congregation rushed out in a panic, and guards came charging in to defend the Duke. The bishops and a few clergy, visibly shaking, were left to finish the ceremony. Aldred, the Anglo-Saxon Chronicle says, refused to place the crown on William's head without a special oath, sworn on the Bible: that he would govern the nation as well as the best of the kings before him, if they were faithful to him. The new King himself, for the first time in his life, was seen to be trembling: but with what emotion nobody knows.

England

New Year's Eve

'The effect of war in this affair was trifling,' William of Malmesbury wrote about sixty years later; 'it was brought about by the secret and wonderful counsel of God; for the Anglo-Saxons never again, in any general battle, made a struggle for liberty, as if the whole strength of England had fallen with Harold.' In twentieth-century terms, he might have said that the conquest was far more psychological than military. The Battle of Hastings was indeed a trifling thing in the downfall of a nation. It need not have been final. Gyrth had known what to do, and one cannot doubt that Harold also knew and would have done it if he had not been distracted by the assault on his conscience. Of all the novel weapons the Conqueror brought, the most effective was not the archery or the horsemen but the papal banner. It was this authority, won by false pretences and granted as a political bargain, that first broke the will of Harold, then of the church, and then of the English people. But I doubt if William used it deliberately: his genius was not so cunningly Machiavellian. More probably it was just another of his strokes of luck that the blessing he had sought for one purpose served him even better for another.

There is no end to the arguments about the ultimate merits of the Norman conquest. It must always be hypothetical to compare the England of the following centuries with what it might have become if the English had been left to develop their own way of life. The consensus is that it was beneficial in the long run. But its benefits were no comfort to the people of 1066, because none of them lived long enough to see them. All they saw was a cruel foreign tyranny. It is reckoned that in the next twenty years two hundred thousand Normans and Frenchmen settled in the country, while at least three hundred thousand English people, one in five of the native population, were killed in William's ravages or starved by the seizure of their farm stock and their land.

Nor did William find much pleasure in his victory. I do not doubt he had hoped to rule a willing peaceful people, but it all went sour on him. He destroyed that hope as soon as he began to promise the lands of England to his followers. The English had offered him the crown, but when they discovered what he intended to do they rebelled again and again. It took him five years of ruthless oppression to put down the active revolts and bring the rest of the country under his power; and apart from the treasures he took home to Normandy, England remained a burden all his life. He never liked the people or the countryside; he gave up the intention he had once expressed of learning the language and spent as much time as he dared in Normandy. Not even an autocrat could have been happy surrounded by people who hated him so bitterly, however obsequious they were to his face. When he was dying, he was said to have repented for the cruelties he knew he had inflicted on them.

Strangely, it was not the mortality itself that most affronted the English; the sudden or lingering deaths could most clearly be seen and accepted as the vengeance of God. Human injustice offended them much more. One can judge this from the Anglo-Saxon Chronicle. One version of it, the Abingdon Chronicle, ended abruptly after recording the Battle of Stamford Bridge, but others were carefully continued all through the awful years that followed; and here one can read the burning resentment of William's greed, his ruinous taxes and his thefts of the treasures of churches and monasteries that Englishmen in moments of piety had made for them and given them in the past; resentment also of the theft of land, practically the whole of the land of England, from its lawful holders, of his oppression of the poor, and his treatment of the revered and respected figures in English life, who were deprived of office, reduced to penury, thrown at his whim into dungeons, chained and manacled, blinded and castrated. People especially resented the eviction of every inhabitant from huge stretches of the countryside to provide new forests for his sport, and the laws protecting the forests which were far more vindictive than those of the English earls and kings. Perhaps most of all they resented the castles the Normans built all over England. There was no external enemy, and William was always strong enough to forbid the private wars that had been the plague of Normandy in the past: the only purpose of the castles was to protect the new landlords against their tenants and provide what England had never had before, a huge number of prisons. The grim stone keeps were a threat to every man and woman in every part of England, and stood as symbols of bondage.

National disaster is always hard to comprehend, and must have been even harder when news spread only from mouth to mouth; so it is better, at the end of the year, to look again at the microcosm where this telling of the story started on New Year's Day, the village of Horstede.

In 1066 the taxable value of Horstede fell by half, from a hundred to fifty shillings. That bleak figure is the only record of the village's disaster. In itself, it signifies that half the village land went out of cultivation; and since the land had never been more than enough to support the people, it implies that many of them had died and the rest continued to live on the edge of starvation.

Horstede is less than twenty miles from the battlefield of Hastings, and eight from the edge of Pevensey harbour. So probably a good many of the able-bodied men of the village set off for the fight and never came back again. But that is not enough to account for the size of its misfortune. There can only have been one cause: some day in that October, a foraging party of soldiers and knights came charging into the little place, which had so seldom seen a stranger and never a foreigner, and slaughtered its beasts and took its stocks of grain – and being the men they were, set fire to what they could not take away, and ravished the women and cut down anyone who was foolish enough to defy them. No village could survive such a raid at that season, just after the harvest was in. When the year began, it was a happy place in its simple fashion: when the year ended, its people were starving to death. And if the soldiery burned the seed corn and killed the draught oxen that drew the ploughs, the survivors of that winter had little hope of a harvest the following year. Twenty years later, the village had still not recovered: its value had only risen from fifty to sixty shillings.

Most of the villages in the valley suffered the same sort of tragedy. Gorde on the other side of the millstream fell from fifty to thirty shillings, Mesewelle up the river fell by half and even Flesching farther away, where the hundred moots had been held, was almost as bad. But Bercham down the river happened not to be raided: it escaped intact, and its value remained the same.

Horstede probably met the sudden disaster with the same fatalism as the rest of the country. A more profound disruption of the village life was still to come. Ulfer the thane had gone, either killed in battle or put in prison or degraded to the status of a cottager, and a new master came riding into the village and installed himself in the house of the thane. His name was Rannulph. In the handout of rewards to William's army he had received a very small estate, so he can scarcely have been a person of much importance – a soldier who had done his duty, or perhaps a servant. Ulfer may have been a good thane or a bad one, a kind man or a mean one: but at least he was English, he spoke the same language, he could preside at the village moot and sit in his proper place in church, he understood the complicated system of rights and custom that kept the place contented, he could listen to people's troubles and join in the feasts, and he was in duty bound to stand up for them in the hundred moot and help them when they needed help. He was one of them, a ruler but also a neighbour. But Rannulph, whatever his character, could not do any of these things. He could not speak the villagers' language and he did not know or probably care how the place had been organized. He had been given it for what he could get out of it. This upstart foreigner, lording it over a tiny place like Horstede, is the measure of England's degradation.

Whatever he did, the village had no appeal. In the world its people knew, every one of the English thanes had gone, and every village had a foreign master. The entire countryside right down to Pevensey, which had been held by Harold, had now been given to Robert of Mortain, William's half-brother, and the forest behind the village now belonged to his other half-brother Odo, a man the English came to detest more than any other. The only place that had not changed hands was the abbey down the river by Lewes, which was still held by the Archbishop of Canterbury – but soon by a new archbishop, Lanfranc himself.

There was nobody anywhere who could help the people of Horstede, nobody they could turn to for advice or justice or under-standing. The whole old comforting system of the moots, where every man had a right to go and speak his mind, had been swept away. Instead, a castle was built directly opposite Horstede on the other side of the river, another at Lewes and another at Pevensey, with dungeons for Englishmen who did not do what they were told.

I have suggested that Horstede was a happy place when the year began because its people felt they could understand their environ-ment and control it: they knew their rights and duties, they knew where they stood. That was the feeling that vanished. The homely village and its fields and woods became a place of doubt and fear and secrecy. Most conquerors deal harshly with the leading men of the countries they dominate and leave the simple people much as they were. But by giving away the land, William brought his conquest into the humblest cottage, and even the children were made to know they were born to a beaten race.

Yet those children, or their children, won a victory in the end. They never became Norman; they remained most stubbornly English, absorbed the invaders and made of the mixture a new kind of Englishness.

Sources

Approximate date	Author	Title
1050	Anon.	Rectitudines Personarum Singularum
1066–67	Anon.	Anglo-Saxon Chronicle
1065–67	Anon.	Vita Aedwardi Regis
1067	Guy of Amiens	Carmen de Hastingae Proelio
1070	William of Jumieges	Gesta Normannorum Ducorum
1072–77	William of Poitiers	Gesta Guillelmi
1080	Anon.	Bayeux Tapestry
1086	Anon.	Domesday Book
1099–1102	Baudri of Bourgeuil	Carmen
1118	Florence of Worcester	Chronicon ex Chronicis
1124	William of Malmesbury	De Gestis Regum Anglorum Vita Wulfstani
1122	Eadmer of Canterbury	Historia Novorum in Anglia
1130	Henry of Huntingdon	Historia Anglorum
1138	Osbert of Clare	Vita Beati Aedwardi Regis Anglorum
1140	Ordericus Vitalis	Historia Ecclesiastica
1161–63	Ailred of Rievaulx	Genalogia Regum Angliae
1160	Robert Wace	Roman de Rou
1216	Anon. of Waltham	Vita Haroldi
1230	Snorri Sturlasson	Heimskringla
1245	Anon. of Westminster	La Estoire de Seint Aedward le Rei

Acknowledgements

I thank the authors and publishers for permission to quote from the translation of the Carmen of Guy of Amiens by Catherine Morton and Hope Muntz (Oxford University Press, 1972), and the translation of Vita Aedwardi Regis by Professor Frank Barlow (Nelson, 1962).

Index

FOR THE BEST IN PAPERBACKS, LOOK FOR THE

In every corner of the world, on every subject under the sun, Penguin represents quality and variety—the very best in publishing today.

For complete information about books available from Penguin—including Puffins, Penguin Classics, and Arkana—and how to order them, write to us at the appropriate address below. Please note that for copyright reasons the selection of books varies from country to country.

In the United Kingdom: Please write to *Dept. JC, Penguin Books Ltd, FREEPOST, West Drayton, Middlesex UB7 0BR.*

If you have any difficulty in obtaining a title, please send your order with the correct money, plus ten percent for postage and packaging, to *P.O. Box No. 11, West Drayton, Middlesex UB7 0BR*

In the United States: Please write to *Consumer Sales, Penguin USA, P.O. Box 999, Dept. 17109, Bergenfield, New Jersey 07621-0120.* VISA and MasterCard holders call 1-800-253-6476 to order all Penguin titles

In Canada: Please write to *Penguin Books Canada Ltd, 10 Alcorn Avenue, Suite 300, Toronto, Ontario M4V 3B2*

In Australia: Please write to *Penguin Books Australia Ltd, P.O. Box 257, Ringwood, Victoria 3134*

In New Zealand: Please write to *Penguin Books (NZ) Ltd, Private Bag 102902, North Shore Mail Centre, Auckland 10*

In India: Please write to *Penguin Books India Pvt Ltd, 706 Eros Apartments, 56 Nehru Place, New Delhi 110 019*

In the Netherlands: Please write to *Penguin Books Netherlands bv, Postbus 3507, NL-1001 AH Amsterdam*

In Germany: Please write to *Penguin Books Deutschland GmbH, Metzlerstrasse 26, 60594 Frankfurt am Main*

In Spain: Please write to *Penguin Books S. A., Bravo Murillo 19, 1° B, 28015 Madrid*

In Italy: Please write to *Penguin Italia s.r.l., Via Felice Casati 20, I-20124 Milano*

In France: Please write to *Penguin France S. A., 17 rue Lejeune, F-31000 Toulouse*

In Japan: Please write to *Penguin Books Japan, Ishikiribashi Building, 2–5–4, Suido, Bunkyo-ku, Tokyo 112*

In Greece: Please write to *Penguin Hellas Ltd, Dimocritou 3, GR–106 71 Athens*

In South Africa: Please write to *Longman Penguin Southern Africa (Pty) Ltd, Private Bag X08, Bertsham 2013*